Field Notes
From The Edge

By the same author:

Herbaceous

Field Notes From The Edge

Journeys Through Britain's Secret Wilderness

PAUL EVANS

LONDON · SYDNEY · AUCKLAND · JOHANNESBURG

1 3 5 7 9 10 8 6 4 2

Rider, an imprint of Ebury Publishing,
20 Vauxhall Bridge Road,
London SW1V 2SA

Rider is part of the Penguin Random House group of companies whose
addresses can be found at global.penguinrandomhouse.com

Line illustrations by Maria Nunzia @Varvera

First published by Rider in 2015. This edition published in 2017

www.eburypublishing.co.uk

A CIP catalogue record for this book is available from the British Library

ISBN 9781846044571

Printed and bound by Clays Ltd, St Ives PLC

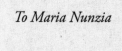

To Maria Nunzia

CONTENTS

INTRODUCTION

As I walk on Wenlock Edge, the wooded limestone escarpment in Shropshire where I was born and where I live, I am constantly reminded of other kinds of 'edge'. The edge between night and day, shadow and light, wood and field, stream and stone, earth and sky, life and death: a constantly changing web of lines. I look out from Wenlock Edge into what Shropshire novelist and poet Mary Webb described as a 'betwixt and between' kind of place. So much has changed since the 1920s when Mary Webb wrote about the Shropshire countryside but I don't have to pretend not to see distant street lights or hear the nag of traffic noise to feel her truth. I look out on a land between England and Wales, betwixt clod-stubborn reality and mysterious shadow. My own story wanders across the margins of this land, stitching the gaps between one thing, one place, one state of mind and another into a life.

Personal stories are about moving from place to place, and these places can be internal as well as out there in the world. Things happen in places which fix them in the memory like a photograph or rub into the imagination like frottage. Sometimes these images remain vivid, sometimes they fade into ghosts. Places have an identity, *genius loci*, a spirit of place. And yet places are dynamic, changeable, moody beings which shape their inhabitants and are shaped by them at the same time. Some places change so much they lose their identity and become placeless, existing only in the presence of a bird, a patch of sunlight or even a thought passing through them.

I like maps, I admire their certainty, but I don't believe them. The Earth has tides of time and space which are never still and attempts to plot their movements lose the plot of their story. I am looking for these shifting boundaries, for thresholds, roads, rivers and Rubicons to cross. I am fascinated by things washed up by such tides or buried, lost, found, hidden or so obvious we never see them.

A lifelong fascination with natural history convinces me that wildlife, wherever it is found, is every bit as wild as in those places we think of as wilderness. Wild is a quality of Nature, a mode of existence and its life is not captured by the managerial language of biodiversity, neither is the wild a destination. Wild Nature is something words are meant to tame. Words define, order, categorise and oppress; wildness is too slippery for that, too indomitable and so it's a fugitive from language. As such, it may appear to be holed up in those remote fastnesses where it can remain defiantly poetic in its sense and emotionally evocative in character. And yet, the more I look, the more I find the wild everywhere, hiding in plain sight, around and within. I am wandering about finding wild lives which inhabit places so wildly marginal their existence is miraculous. To witness these miracles and attempt to articulate them is really the point, if a point is needed, of my journey told here. This travelling is a rather serendipitous, undisciplined, hands-in-pockets sauntering kind of adventure. Through it I am discovering a sense of community with other wild creatures which trespass between boundaries. Through them I am not only redefining the edges around and within me but what I mean by me.

Britain has no wilderness, I am told. Scratch farmers of the Neolithic and forest-clearing axe-men of the Bronze Age began the attrition of what we imagine of the wild wood. In more recent centuries, moorland was purged of people as well as trees for sheep farming and grouse shooting. The lowlands turned into countryside, which, as far as wildlife is concerned is, to use a technical term, 'knackered', as are the coastal waters and seas. Something like wilderness is restricted to cliffs, estuaries and dreams. Elsewhere in the world, the traditional idea of wilderness has long been compromised by people who go in search of it. Whether on a quest for an earthly paradise, the healing of wounds inflicted by modern society, an ecologically authentic sense of self or a more dangerous adventure overcoming ancestral challenges, wilderness tourists make demands on Nature's indifference, arguably more so than those who have lived there for countless centuries. Despite appeals to re-connect the urbanised, industrialised consumer with Nature and think differently about the non-human world, the war against Nature intensifies. This is not a war first prosecuted by modernists, it is one which began with the origins of civilisation when a fear of Nature I describe as ecophobia became a fundamental part of human existence.

This fear persists and, even with the rise of environ-mentalism, it is responsible for atrocities to Nature as brutal as any war of these mad times. Floods, droughts, storms, desertification, melting ice caps and tundra, oceanic pollution, atmospheric pollution, deforestation, urban sprawl, intensive agriculture, over-fishing, globalisation, species extinction: how sickening the litany of destruction and its anxieties has become. However, this wave of nausea masks the unnoticed creation of new kinds of wild. Degraded habitats, swarms of 'invasive' species, novel pathogens and diseases: a Nature we don't like is replacing the Nature we do.

The creativity of Nature lies in the old chaos, it surges from Earth's fault lines. Life leaks from the cracks and not from the wishful thinking of balance that people have struggled to engineer. This is not a good thing for those who cling to a pastoral vision of Nature and the duty of stewardship to manage it for the good of humanity. Although this is a romantic impulse I recognise in myself, I now know that game is up. 'Nature is good,' says philosopher Alan Holland, 'even if it's not good for us.' In a time of environmental and social crisis, there is a risk of taking myself too seriously and I apologise (sort of) for a pervading sense of melancholy in this story. There are, however, surprises, discoveries and excitements which bring moments of real joy to this journey and, I hope, a sense of humour which appreciates the absurdity of our plight. Even in this terrible undoing of the world, I feel a dark wonder for what will replace it.

This journey into Britain's secret wilds begins when I resolve to stop looking for them. One thing leads to another and the wild finds me. Decisions about where to go and when are made more by happenstance and random coincidence than planning. The only conscious thing I do is to keep notebooks of writing in the field. These field notes link back to others because, as a writer, journalist, broadcaster, conservationist and gardener, I've been very fortunate to have done a lot of wandering around looking at wildlife and landscapes and writing about it.

When I begin to fit these field notes together, what emerges is a journey through Britain's changing landscapes. From Ice Age caves to suburbia I scramble about in the ruins of utopian dreams and dystopian nightmares, picking through the strandline, ducking in and out of shadows between wood and heath, listening to the thinking swarms of life, standing in a ghost forest, haunting the dusk. I meet extraordinary people and learn from their journeys. In the strange yet ordinary ridgeways, shingle spits, fens, woods, streets and ditches, the land's stories find me. All I do is splice together what I've learned from natural history, literature, art, philosophy and folklore with raw intuitions and experience, to describe a Nature that is inspiring yet intimidating, miraculous yet mundane, sacred, wasteland.

This is a work of dark wonder for what is happening to the land in which my story lives. It is a journey with no idea where it's going, no ideological compass and no map on which the secret wilds can be plotted. These are a few field notes from along the edge between the fear and love of Nature, without which there is nothing.

I.
RIDGE

A long narrow hilltop or escarpment, mountain range or watershed; an elevated crest; a raised strip between furrows or troughs; the junction of upward-sloping surfaces.

CHIFFCHAFF

I take the path from the main road at the top of the dingle which begins in a tangle of nettle and bramble at a broken stile. It shoves into the wood between a field called the Yeld – an old name for wasteland – and the edge of a worked-out quarry. This was a path for quarry workers, lime-burners, farm labourers and a thoroughfare for packhorse strings, drovers and travellers. *Chiff-chaff . . . chiff-chaff . . .* the two-beat call of a chiffchaff echoes the left–right of old nailed boots on stone.

For all I know, this bird may have spent the winter in Lyme Regis or Burkina Faso. Some chiffchaffs migrate to and from West Africa and some stay close but this one returns each year to a crab-apple tree at the wood's edge. These birds belong to a genus, which includes the willow warbler and wood warbler, called *Phylloscopus* from *phyllon*, meaning leaf and *skopeo*, to see. They are small birds, leaf-like, with a plumage of greens, browns and yellows, spending most of their time foraging for butterfly and moth caterpillars in the tree canopy. They each carry a light band above the eye which marks them out as seers, watchful creatures looking into the life of the trees, seeing the way of old paths over the woods through the sky from Africa, across Europe to here. They are the seeing-leaves.

Unlike other warblers with enchanting, liquid music, chiffchaffs have this two-note walking song, quick and sharp and I follow it on the old road, which is barely my boot's width today. Less travelled – because the places of work it linked have gone and the settlements it served have roads for very different traffic – the path is no more than a rut through woods. I keep it open. This is where woodcock flared into a winter sky; starving deer stripped bark off ivy; spring poked through late snow with purple orchids; a fox hid the corpse of a lamb; dead man's finger – the black wizened digit of fungus – pointed from a fallen branch. The path is a linear progression between, away from and towards things: the broken stile at the road, stone walls, limestone cliffs with polypody ferns, a rabbit warren on steep quarry spoil, ash trees along the Yeld's medieval hedgebank, the slope under a fallen hawthorn up to the wood, the broken stile at the other end opening onto a lane. These landmarks along this path lead to other places, other paths. As such this is part of a web of journeying for me and other people, birds, mammals, insects and the flow of plants and fungi. And yet it is a somewhere in itself. Its nature is to travel and be travelled and what happens along it is shaped by what is travelling and how. Although that may be the nature of all paths, it does not capture the unique nature of this path.

A narrow space, like a crease in fabric, gathers me into the ordinary yet extraordinary life in the margins between fields, woods and quarries. As with ancient processional ways through the land walked by ancestors practising religious rites, the path is a preparation for a different way of thinking about and experiencing the world. What the walker started off thinking at the road stile may not be what they end up thinking at the lane stile. The path becomes a fluid state of mind between, away from and towards other thoughts, moods, intuitions, ideas. It is a state of disorientation like that which occurs in rituals, which alter the state of mind before, during and after the ritual.

To walk can be a ritual in itself. It may be to get to work or the shops or to visit; it may be to take a gun, the dog, watch wildlife, forage herbs; it may be to think, to meditate, to commune; it may be for exercise, habit, exploration, fun; it may be any or none of these things – it may be just a walk. And yet the walk changes the walker.

The act of walking is a performance: one-foot-in-front-of-the-other, the act of journeying between and through places stirs up the past and brings it into the present. This may not be what the lime-burners thought – untying their masks of blood-soaked rags from breathing quicklime – but it is my performance to walk this way thinking of them. The performance is not about recreating the past or hope or atonement, it is simply to join the rhythm of returning workers, funeral processions, strolling lovers, midnight flits, hiding and seeking. Pathways are full of footprints. I tread on the unseen impressions that ghosts leave behind. They tread on mine.

The path is a transition between the state of mind before the walk and the one after it and represents a threshold between them. But instead of being crossed, the path is walked; I travel along it, threading a borderline between, away from and towards different mental states and physical places, becoming transitory, liminal. The path leads to a network of transitions: a web of connections between different states of mind and different places, like cracks in the pavement, thresholds not necessarily crossed but a kind of becoming, a liminal edge in which the ritual may never be complete. *Chiff-chaff . . . chiff-chaff . . .* chants the bird from an ash tree, wrapped in his own ritual. A way of thinking about this is what Heidegger called, in *The Thinker as Poet*, 'the utopism of a half-poetic intellect': it may represent the worst of philosophical muddles, it may be romantically delusional but it does describe how I experience wandering among such extraordinary wonders of the living world as if my life were enchanted.

Up at the other end, another broken stile opens onto a narrow lane. A buzzard mews through a loop of air rising over woods and the Yeld. A wren flies across the lane, singing a five-second burst of little bells falling down a well, into a hazel thicket at the entrance to another wood once called Tomlinson's Hill. Over a hundred years ago, this was a quarry with a kiln that supplied lime to the iron foundries at Coalbrookdale down the river. During its years of operation, Tomlinson's Hill was decapitated and replaced by a ruinous landscape of cliffs, pits and pudding-basin spoil heaps. The foundries made the cast-iron skeleton for the industrial age, sucking limestone, iron-ore, coal and timber from the hinterland around their furnaces. They went cold and industry moved on. Coalbrookdale, Ironbridge and the Severn Gorge, where my mother's family were from, became a museum, a World Heritage Site, a shrine to the insane alchemy that is still burning up the world. *Birthplace of the Industrial Revolution* its sign reads but it will never admit to being the *Birthplace of Global Warming*. Derelict places like Tomlinson's Hill are collateral damage of the Industrial Revolution and forgotten.

Since its abandonment, Tomlinson's Hill quarry has been recolonised by mosses, limestone meadow plants, gauntly enigmatic hawthorns and the massed spear-rattle of ash trees. This post-industrial process of natural succession filled in the bare stone and rubble left by quarrying with life from the unworked margins which bordered it. In the last fifty years, agricultural intensification has rubbed out much of the surrounding wildlife and so this little wood with its glades flickering with meadow brown and silver-washed fritillary butterflies is now an island of dynamic ecological change in an ossified countryside. One day the reverse process will happen and, like osmosis, the sterile fields will be colonised by life seeping back out through the porous membranes of the quarry wood. Inside, its veiny mesh of paths is travelled by deer, foxes, badgers and rabbits holed up like outlaws.

The first time I came across this little wood I had no idea what it was. A right of way from the lane was marked on the map. I took it. The path led through overhanging hawthorns and hazels with old straight stems and wound around mounds, pits and limestone outcrops. Back then, there was a small field grazed by donkeys but that's covered in bramble and briar now. There were still open grassy glades where jewel-like flowers of pyramidal orchid and cobalt specks of milkwort grew in summer. The strange humps and gaunt old thorns gave the wood an otherworldly feel. It was a sunny day and as I explored the twists and turns of paths made by animals through the wood, I heard the sound of children playing and a woman talking and realised I had stumbled into someone's back garden. I thought the house must face the lane but I couldn't quite see it; the garden of the house must be just beyond some scrub where I could hear kids running around. Not wanting to startle anyone and sure that I'd strayed onto private property, I backed off quietly. A week or so later, curious to find out where the house was, I walked down to the lane to investigate. There was nothing there. No house, no garden. At least, there hadn't been a house or garden there for over fifty years. There was evidence of one though: a few mossed-over piles of bricks, a patch of cyclamen, a fallen laburnum tree, a couple of conifers and some ornamental currant bushes with bright pink flowers.

At the wood's furthest edge is another stile now replaced by an aluminium kissing-gate. Passing there is always a surprise as the viewer is suddenly thrown into the view. The Wrekin hill looms up 1,000 feet to the north; like buzzard flight, the eye drops across woodland 300 feet below and then north-west through Severn Vale; past the sandstone stumbling-block hills of the Shropshire Plain and over the green wall of hillsides across the Welsh border 35 miles away behind smoke from the chipboard factory at Chirk and over hazy summits of the Berwyn mountains beyond. Facing west, into the sky and a suddenness of space, the grand sweep of landscape after the close intimacy of the wood is both disorientating and uplifting.

I find being thrown into the prospect evokes an unexpected feeling towards the world. It's as if I've seen behind a hoax, and after being led through myopic corridors of the wood am suddenly let into the secret that the world is huge. This is something like the tale Colin Wilson, in *The Outsider* (1956), tells of Wordsworth's explanation to Thomas De Quincy about how he wrote his poetry. Wordsworth had his ear to the road, listening for the rumble of the mail cart from Keswick. He stood up suddenly and at the same moment caught sight of the evening star, which appeared intensely beautiful to him. Wordsworth claimed what he saw immediately after relaxing his concentration on something that had nothing to do with poetry was so beautiful and surprising it inspired him to write. I'm not sure if my own concentration on the wood is poetic or not but everything has something to do with poetry here. This walk is, like the chiffchaff, a kind of seeing but the abrupt change in scale when suddenly confronted by the view is shaking. My shrinking in size and significance before the sweeping landscape is humbling and invigorating, an altered state. It always takes a few giddy seconds to adjust to the space.

On the boundary between wood and field, looking into the landscape, height and distance diminish the impact of human labour. Here there is more closeness to the weather than to the industrialised world cast from Coalbrookdale's foundries. It is the liberating sense of freedom that comes from the lie of the land and breadth of the sky that sets the senses soaring. Feeling the world like this is not to have it explained but presented through the marvels and mysteries of the living world – the flight of birds through sunset, the rise of mountains, the course of rivers. This kind of numinous experience is not dependent on a belief or faith in anything supernatural or divine but nevertheless I experience a feeling of sacredness.

An ordinary, vernacular kind of sacred is not diminished because it hasn't been constructed in the monumental forms of religious thought and tradition. Instead it's a personally intuitive, emotional, psychological knowing of how Nature matters. It remains unspoken, a recognition of a sacredness in Nature which is indifferent to us. Such a feeling cannot be conditional; I think it comes from love.

What remains of Tomlinson's Hill and the strange little wood of wonders it has become opens onto this view across Shropshire into Wales at the northern end of Wenlock Edge. To the south, farmland rises like the slack of a wave up to a line of tall beech and lime trees. Beneath them and invisible from here, is the drop of the scarp: a near vertical slope with cliffs which, apart from being cut through by roads, forms the longest unbroken ribbon of woodland in England, stretching nearly 20 miles from the birthplace of the Industrial Revolution in the Severn Gorge to the gateway to the Welsh Marches in Craven Arms. This wave of bone is made from fossilised remains of creatures which drew calcium from the waters of a warm shallow sea to protect their fragile bodies 425 million years ago. Dragged by plate tectonics from the southern hemisphere over eons, the Edge stands poised, ready to flood across the lowlands and crash into the mountains of Wales.

Walking along the axis of the Edge from north-east to south-west – where the gentle rise of the dip slope meets the plunge down the scarp, where fields meet woods, east meets west, shelter meets the storm – I follow a liminal line. It's a line along which the ritual dances of speckled wood butterflies tie and undo aerial knots of strobing wings; where ravens fly like sharpening stones honing a blade, yelling *kronk!* at the wind; where noctule bats stream from holes in old beech trees after dusk to slalom sonically through the night air. There are times when walking the Edge is to be the Edge walking.

A queen flies wildly pursued by the swarm. Before it catches up with her and they crash together into one buzzing orgiastic mass in the linden tree, there is a hunt in which every bee is magnetised by the same compelling passion. Like the swarm, the Edge line chases a fugitive love across the land. It is an eternal hunt: an infatuation pulsing through bees, butterflies, ravens and bats; propelling me along the Edge in pursuit of an unknown object of desire; carried on a wave that surges north-west with the weight of England behind it. But like all loves, which by their very wild nature cannot be explained or reasoned with, there are dark moments, disturbing passions.

The path doglegs from the Edge line to cross the main Shrewsbury road, steering clear of Edge Top above the old quarry cutting carved for the road by Napoleonic prisoners of war. It is fenced off. *Chiff-chaff . . . chiff-chaff . . .* chants the bird from a tree. Each syllable is separated by a tiny axis of silence, a split between realities: one note for this world, one for another; between them runs the Edge. I listen for the silence. All the time, the bird is watching: the field behind Edge Top, weedy, unsettled, flitting with finch charms and moths; it's called Gallows Tree Leasowe. High above traffic labouring up the bank below the cliffs, against old wych elm suckers from a once-huge tree, the view opens to hills beyond the plain, to silver towns and bolts of sunlight through gathering clouds. There, a land spreads out towards the north-west glowing with a visionary light for the final moments of prisoners brought here in chains long ago. Left, right, left, right . . . the footsteps of the damned. Boom, boom, boom, boom . . . the drumbeat march to the gallows. *Chiff-chaff, chiff-chaff . . .* the seeing-leaves watch everything. The swarm goes quiet; the crowd holds its breath – snap! The rope creaks as the condemned dance upon the Tree of Misadventure.

LAPWING

The view from Gallows Tree Leasowe on Edge Top, high above the road cutting, looking north-west towards Severn Vale, the plain and far hills, was the last impression on the retinas of the condemned. As the rope snapped taut, the feet kicked empty air, the body twitched and loosed its fluids, the mind fixed an image of a land which, with a squint, persists today. Within that same space are ghostly images of absent beings that left a curse bound forever to this place.

There were once lapwings in the fields of this view. Thousands and thousands of lapwings – piebald white, black and iridescent green birds with plumed crests, 'hornpies'; with a tumbling flight through the air, 'flopwings'; screaming their eerie cry, 'peewits', '*pee-wit, pee-wit, peewit!*'. In Old English *hleapewince*, 'leaper-winker', meant to leap and 'wink', may come from the black on white patches of the underwing which, when dancing in the air, looks like winking; it also means totter, waver and move rapidly. These birds were by the fourteenth century, according to Chaucer's 'Parliament of Fowles', the 'false lapwynge, ful of treacherye'. The received explanation for the birds' treachery lay in the lapwing's strategy of feigning injury by dragging a wing on the ground, luring potential predators away from eggs or chicks hiding in the grass. But lapwings also feigned madness: the leaper-winkers flung themselves into the air erratically, to tumble, flounce and mug in a display of wild exuberance, mobbing intruders as if crazy; a mock insanity masking a calculated communal mind which earned such flocks the collective noun: a *deceit* of lapwings. The Greeks called them *polyplagkos*, 'luring on deceitfully'.

> From the hagg and hungry goblin
> That into raggs would rend ye,
> And the spirit that stands by the naked man
> In the Book of Moones – defend ye!
> (*Tom O'Bedlam, anonymous ballad c.1600*)

The hangings on Gallows Tree Leasowe were first recorded during the turbulent 1540s, just after the dissolution of the monasteries. Thomas Butler, himself a deposed abbot who became the first vicar of Wenlock, entered the executions of criminals into his register in Latin together with accounts of the lives of ex-inmates from the monasteries, visits by dignitaries, the burials of organ players, bell-ringers, stonemasons, brewers and sextons. It was during this period when, with the power of the religious houses gone, their lands were parcelled up and distributed among supporters of the king and those powerful enough to claim land by force. These new patterns of manorial estates, yeomen farms and abandoned villages reshaped the Tudor landscape to form the hedged-in countryside, much modified but clearly recognisable nearly five hundred years later spreading out across the plain below the Edge. With land reform came laws to control all life on it – everything from crows to kingfishers – and a duty of every parish to support farming and keep food prices down by persecuting wildlife. This helped the ascendancy of those managing both an efficient war against Nature and against the wild corners of the human spirit aroused by religious ferment. Like gamekeeper's larders – the fences on which were hung the corpses of vermin as evidence of duty and as examples to all villainous crows, moles and polecats – the gallows tree answered many questions of belief, allegiance and doubt.

Alice Glaston was hanged from the gallows tree here in 1545. She was eleven years old. Butler's register records only her name, age, her parish – Little Wenlock – and the fact she was hanged with three others. This made Alice Glaston the youngest woman hanged in England. Because there are no references to her crime, her trial or her life, she floats free from history, free to inhabit the imagination, a spirit of this place taking any shape.

To me, Alice belongs to an older country. She was sacrificed at the beginning of the world we recognise today. She haunts a threshold on the edge of a more distant past that had mostly perished in the Black Death. After Alice, laws reshaped the rural landscape, ordered labour, institutionalised poverty, outlawed wildlife, industrialised farming and accused the wise of witchcraft. After Alice, the poor surviving at the margins of society feigned madness to appeal for charity, using the old lapwing strategy the Greeks had a proverbial phrase for, 'more beseeching than a lapwing' to describe the 'sturdy' (artful) beggars, vagabonds, Mad Mauds – fallen women (Maud from Maudlin, the English spelling of Magdalene) – and Tom O'Bedlams – refugees from the Bethlehem (Bedlam) asylums personified in the anonymous ballad first written down around 1600.

These were a deceit of lapwings, taxing, mugging for alms or tribute, *pee-wit, pee-wit!*

Who, in the old ballad, cursed Tom O'Bedlam? Who drove him mad? Who does he call to for help? According to the medieval almanac of the supernatural called the Book of Moons, the 'naked man' is Hermes the magician. Who, in the ballad, is the spirit that stands before Hermes? The spirit here is no hag or goblin but Alice Glaston. Her execution laid a curse on this land and it is she who speaks through the lunatics: the leaping, winking lapwings who rise treacherously against the powerful arbiters of the law; madness their only defence; doomed. This story returns to the land with the people poor mad John Clare called 'clowns', the yokels who leer out of history like a shelf of Toby jugs: sly, deceitful, irreverent and superstitious – my people, buried long ago under a sod which itself hardly survives today.

Relics of Alice's world now appear as tricks of the light. From the windmill, when the sun is low against the southern downs, shadows pick out stepped ridges which follow the contours. These 'strip lynchets' may have begun in the Bronze Age, 4,000 years ago; the soil ploughed across the slopes slumping downhill or else deliberately built. They formed narrow terraces of 'risers' and 'treads' over centuries of cultivation. Lynchets – from the Saxon *hlinc*, cultivation terrace – may have been part of Celtic or Saxon fields or they may have been constructed in the Middle Ages but they were certainly used until Alice's time. On these flights up the hill, each tread, each step, is a 'land' in itself. Not much wider than the ox pulling the plough here, each improbable land belonged to a family for a few rows of grain to sell to the miller. Take out the tithe to the Church, the rent to the manor, the tax to the king, and what's left had to keep the wolf from the door. On lynchets around the West Country, down the Wessex Ridgeway to the terraces across Europe and Asia, the poor and their animals hacked out a living from the hillsides, engineered the water flow, modified the soil, carved the rhythm of their lives up and down these stairs between earth and sky.

Other shadowlands on the Edge are what remain of ridge and furrow. Seen as corrugations in fields, they were formed by a pattern of ploughing which created a broad, raised strip, the ridge or a 'land', separated by a ditch or furrow a furlong – furrow-long – in length. Like the lynchets, the ridge and furrow method grew grain and other crops in the medieval open field system. Sometimes, individual 'lands' were owned by individual families. Now they are mostly ploughed out by modern agriculture and its huge, deep ploughs. The ridge and furrow is as anachronistic as deserted villages, evacuated during the Black Death. They are the ghost lands.

Lapwings love the plough. They nest closest to the earth in a shallow scraped by their own feet on ploughed soil among crops. At Easter, they lay a single clutch of olive-green and dark brown speckled eggs. Unlike birds such as swallows, which will keep laying eggs even if they're taken away, lapwings only lay four and that's it: four seasons, four elements, four cardinal points of the compass, four – the numerological symbol for earth and home. The Saxon tradition of exchanging eggs at *Eostur-monath*, searching the fields for them in the Easter egg hunt, is lured by the birds into a liminal space between the sacred and the profane.

Lapwing eggs had always been an important part of the rural diet. They became particularly fashionable to Victorians and, with their sin of enthusiasm, they collected them in bulk. In 1845, a single egger in Norfolk snaffled up 160 dozen (1,920) lapwing eggs in one day. This kind of plunder was bound to affect the population and had to be controlled by the Lapwing Act of 1926, although the subsequent increase in population may have had more to do with the agricultural depression of that time.

The humbug-camouflaged chicks are born precocious and reckless. Shakespeare wrote in *Hamlet* of a man going unprepared and overly self-confident: *Horatio*: 'This lapwing runs away with the shell on his head' but a lapwing bursts from the egg with functional sense organs and a mental development, which in a matter of hours can respond to the kind of complexities of life that takes weeks or months in many other birds and certainly years in ourselves. From the bare earth lapwings run to cattle-grazed wet meadow, moor, heath, salt marsh, airfield, sewage farm or gravel pit to feed on insects, spiders, earthworms, snails, millipedes or woodlice.

The lapwing community, the *deceit*, sticks together. Feigning injury to draw the gullible away from defenceless chicks or, in sufficient numbers, scaring off trespassers with a display of fearless Tom O'Bedlam craziness, binds lapwing society, as does journeying. Lapwings travel together in huge numbers. During the winter, some British lapwings head for Ireland, the Iberian Peninsula or North Africa but most stay close to home where they are joined by migrants. Between half and three-quarters of the lapwing population of western and central Europe move in to the sloshing fields, fens, moors, marshes and mires of Britain and Ireland for the winter. Lapwing culture is acutely sensitive to changes in the weather. The birds anticipate storms and move en-masse to avoid them. In February 1900, a great trail of lapwings 3 miles long flew over the Scilly Isles from the north-west. I heard a story about a strange cloud picked up by wartime radar moving south across Britain and getting bigger and bigger. It turned out to be lapwings flying before a storm. They flew as far as western France, rested until the storm died out at home then flew back. In December 1978 at Shoreham-by-Sea, West Sussex, 40,000 lapwings arrived to escape a storm. Such gatherings have not been seen since.

From Edge Top, the view Alice would have seen in her final moments on the Gallows Tree is almost devoid of lapwings now. There is a long straight road heading towards Shrewsbury and just where it kinks out of sight behind woods before Cross Houses is Venus Pool. The flooded gravel workings are where the last of the peewits gather like the remnants of some forgotten subculture clinging to its reckless and beautiful lost youth. There were once hundreds in the fields between there and the River Severn but during a generation they have been reduced to little more than a handful. The estimated decline in the lapwing population in the wider region of the West Midlands is around 52 per cent. Here in Shropshire it is over 80 per cent and most of that decline has happened only in the last twenty years. Another collective noun for lapwing is, with a terrible irony, a *desert*.

Farmers I have spoken to deny that so much has changed in the countryside over the last couple of decades to cause such a catastrophic collapse of the lapwing population.

They claim they're doing pretty much the same things they always have. They remember when those cutting the fields would stop the tractor to pick up lapwing chicks and move them out of harm's way and regret that may not happen any more. But a switch to ploughing in spring instead of winter, pesticides, synthetic chemicals, loss of fallow land, drainage, livestock density, walkers with dogs, increased predators such as crows and huge machines cutting the heads off chicks can plunge an already weakened population on the edge into terminal decline. There are farmland conservation schemes attempting to recreate conditions for lapwings but they are pathetically few and far between. Shame.

The horned bird; the crowned bird, suspected by the sixteenth-century occult philosopher Cornelius Agrippa of being royal; the bird Leviticus lists as unclean and taboo, together with eagle, raven, barnacle goose, heron, which all had affiliations with non-Semitic deities; the bird the Qur'an claims is the keeper of King Solomon's secrets; the bird Robert Graves in *The White Goddess* (1948) believes to be the guardian of the secret identity of gods . . . this bird stands at Venus Pool with the last few of its kind. They are no longer a deceit; isolated from each other, they stand motionless in the rain at water's edge, lost in their secrets.

2.
FRONT

The ground towards a real or imagined enemy;
the outward appearance; the promenade of a seaside resort;
to confront, meet, oppose; an organised group.

SPUME

. . . . EME . . S are the only letters of 'amusements' left above glass doors behind the sandbags. Inside the arcade, the lights on the gaming machines are still on, I suppose for ghost punters, playing the lurid mathematics of one-arm-banditry. Next door, the Golden Sands is boarded up. All the identical green caravans are empty, except one. On the seafront, a red warning flag, shredded like a forgotten socialist republic, thrashes from its pole above three cars, steamed up, rocking in the wind bansheeing from the sea.

One car leaves, another arrives. Someone gets out, suddenly thumped by a gust and a bucket of rain, trying to look casual leaning on the rail. The waves are steely green, their ridges flying spindrift. All down the bay from way out to sea they come charging ashore, north-east to south-west, terrifyingly beautiful. A stone's throw from the promenade is an island built to stumble the waves before they strike the front. Behind black rocks the sea smashes its endlessly renewed face and on a narrow causeway connecting sea wall and breakwater, two gulls lift and drop and a lone sanderling stands watching them. The rail-leaner lets go and crabs back to the car: sandwiches, flask of tea, turns the radio up.

The sea is so far in, too far. A spring tide fills the estuary between mountains to wedge them apart and let the uncoiling thing from the ocean ram up the crack. For now, the shingle holds the shore together and the gale screams overhead and hums through the rail. In the cars they watch the rain ease and waves diminish and a young couple in matching red wellingtons walk along the front chased by an empty plastic bottle. In a few minutes they return, resolutely in step against the wind, frightened off by spume.

The promenade ends in steps down to the shingle, now hardly a span from the waves, and an outcrop of rocks where a white cloud has formed. The wind whips it up in gobs and spits it landwards like firefighting foam on a crashed aeroplane. The spume may have been caused by oil discharged at sea or stormwater full of sewage and detergent but this has a meringuey lightness which suggests it was created by phytoplankton or algal blooms. A microscopic alga, *Phaeocystis globosa*, sometimes free-moving with its own flagella, can also create colonies, brown scum, thousands of ball-shaped cells surrounded by a mucus membrane of carbohydrate gel. *Phaeocystis* has a globally fundamental role cycling carbon and sulphur in the oceans. In spring, influenced by high levels of nitrogen and other pollutants which nourish phytoplankton, these blooms become so vast they are visible from space satellites. Caught in storms, wave turbulence churns the proteins, lignins and lipids in the algal colony's gel into foaming agents, trapping air in the surf zone where the bubbles of spume stick to each other through surface tension and are blown ashore.

Red-welly couple are heads down into the wind, unable to stand upright. At first, they think the spume looks like fun, bubble-bath, disco foam. They will take photos of each other playing with it, chucking it around like snow. Remember Ibiza? Well this is Wales, in the gales! At last, here is something to break the spell of the storm in this little necrophiliac seaside town; something happily random to show their friends. Then they find themselves in it.

The spume is animated: creeping across rocks, crouching in the corner by the steps and sliding under the rail to pulse like snaking musculature across the path. White but slightly soiled, not pure like spindrift, it is searching them out. Clumps of flob in the wind, catching on their clothes, eyelashes and lips; it begins to repulse them. They shut their mouths and hold their breaths because they can't make out what the substance is: something with all the qualities of mattress stuffing, mousse, fog, fat, fleece, spit, spunk, spray. Is it toxic? Is it alive?

Phaeocystis, sea, storm, shit, washed from land or dumped by ships, climate change warming the oceans: spume is more than coincidence. Indifferent like snow, intentional like a swarm, each delicate bubble encased in a meniscus of water and algal slime is attached to others to form a mass, but containing what? In the news, a massive algal foam on an Australian beach concealed venomous sea snakes. Here, is it only air? Inside each bubble there may be microscopic fragments of plankton rattling around. Inside each tiny film may be the kind of evolutionary turmoil in which eukaryotic cells – the ones with a nucleus – formed from Frankenstein bits of older organisms shaken together in foaming storms 2 billion years ago. Each bubble is an evolutionary possibility; the stuff of tempests; a quantum state between nothingness; a life. And then . . . pop!

Red-welly couple are disgusted and struggle back along the front against the wind. They don't see the gull cruising at shoulder height also against the wind but with such indolent ease like a watchful mugger. They don't see the clouds fracture and a bolt of sunlight hit the waves. They don't speak their fear to each other but push on to the public toilets where they split up and even in the cold, stinky dankness of the bogs, find relief in hot water washing the spume's potentiality from their hands and faces. What will become of them, now they've been contaminated, impregnated . . . turned?

COMMON GULL

There are two cars left under the thrashing red flag on the front. They are still rocking in the wind but the rain has stopped, clouds have sundered and there is golden enamel across the green waves. In one of the cars, the small blue one, a woman turns the radio off because the news reports make her feel nauseous. She opens the window a crack and lights a cigarette. She wonders where the intimacy of the couple walking past went to and how their matching wellingtons, which looked like charming engagement presents when they walked along the front, now look ridiculous as they walk back. She knows that feeling. Salt spray covers her windscreen and across it, with barely a movement, a gull appears to glide magically into the wind.

How does it do that? This one gull, without appearing to make any effort, flies into a wind against which she struggles to open the car door, in which she can hardly stand up. Where are all the other gulls? It drops out of sight and a moment later reappears to do the same thing, over and over again. Why does it do that? First time round it seems fascinating and beautiful as if the bird is being playful, enjoying its skill in such a wind but there is something about the repetition and persistence of this action which unsettles her. An obsession, an idée fixe; the gull has discovered a way through the wind, sliding down an invisible chute but it cannot stop.

She hears the wind in the window gap whistle and whine and listens to a demon whispering to the gull. *This life of yours: you will have to repeat it forever; there will be nothing new; every pain, every joy, every thought, everything big and small in your life will come back to you in the same order as before and for all eternity you will be but a feather balancing in the storm. Will you despair and curse me or will you now become yourself and live to love nothing else?* She reverses out of the car park quickly and drives away east, following the storm which has just reached towns on the other side of the mountains.

SANDERLING

And now there's only our car left under the flag on the front. The storm has careered off but the wind is still strong. The sky is silver and blue and grey. The waves have settled down but are persistent, white-topped, pushing relentlessly at the sliver of exposed shingle bank where a lone sanderling stands watching. Flecks of spume and spray of spindrift fill the air and it looks as if the tide will not turn. Damn. Out there, underwater, is the forest.

Recent storms have scoured the beach, peeling back layers of sand and pebbles and dumping it further down the bay. This has, like a conjuror's trick, revealed a forest floor over ten thousand years old. We have come to walk between the stumps of birch, pine, alder and oak as did wolf, bear, elk and auroch at the end of the Ice Age. If the sanderling had been watching from the edge of the sunken forest, it would be several miles further out to sea now. That forest reduced to an edge 4 miles along the bay and 50 feet wide. Sea level rise and stories of a tidal wave submerged the forest of a mythical land and although it comes to light in places occasionally after storms along the coast, this is the first time here in living memory. We have come to meet the ghost of an Ice Age forest before it is covered over again.

Sanderlings still live for half the year in the ice age. Long-distance migrants, breeding in the high Arctic of Svalbard, Siberia, Canada and Greenland during the summer, the birds only return here for winter. This one may have come from Iceland, even Baffin Bay. Like the mountain hare, the stoat in ermine and the ptarmigan, the sanderling wears winter white. On the summer tundra its plumage is brown, brick-red and it is aggressively territorial but here, on the long sandy beaches of Cardigan Bay, some snow and ice memory turns it white, pale grey and gregarious. Sanderlings have a split, north–south personality. When the forest was here, northern Britain was buried under an ice cap. As the Arctic shrank north around the pole, the sanderlings followed the tundra to breed but brought their young back every year to run the wave-edge here. They remind us of *our* Arctic: the last of fifteen Ice Ages ended 10,000 years ago in Britain, when we followed reindeer herds to their calving grounds, where sanderlings laid their eggs, long before we came here to play slot machines or sit in cars drinking tea. White as spume and spindrift, the sanderling inhabits a wavelength between the ice and the forest and the front.

With no hind toe, these dapper little waders usually dart on their pins along the beach like cartoon birds at a manic pace, pausing to pick worms and crablings as they rise through sand under lapping waves or rummage for larvae in seaweed twists. Oddly, this sanderling is alone and still. Its life is pending. It can't dodge these heavy waves smacking into stones and it's too cold to find spiders. Like us, it stands waiting vainly for the tide to go out and something wonderful to appear. Stories of lost forests have been told for centuries. Richard James wrote in 1636:

> How many thousands of theis trees now stand,
> Black broken on their rootes, which once drie land
> Did cover, whence turfs Neptune yeelds to showe
> He did not always to theis borders flowe.

In Welsh deluge myths, Cantre'r Gwaelod – The Bottom Hundred – is a tract of land which ran down Cardigan Bay between Bardsey and Ramsey Islands spreading 20 miles out to sea. Another, and perhaps the same place, is the plain of Maes Gwyddno which, in the twelfth-century Black Book of Carmarthen, drowned in a flood leaving bells to chime underwater in times of peril. Under this popular seaside, in coastal waters I paddled in as a child, lie relics of an ancient land.

The Sarnau are moraine causeways of clays, gravels and stones dumped by glaciers, stretching at 90 degrees to the coast far out to sea between the four rivers entering Cardigan Bay. Submerged remains of forest and bog are scattered all around the bay and may well have extended along the Sarnau, like a massive ridge and furrow system before the seas rose. On the beaches, 5,000-year-old stumps of oak, pine, birch, willow and hazel are often exposed at Ynyslas, preserved by acidic anaerobic conditions and just last week Bronze Age fish traps and a boardwalk made of hazel were found there. In the submerged forest, oak stumps 6 feet wide have been discovered and the ones opposite the amusement arcade on the front may be Mesolithic.

The uncovering of the sunken forest is not like archaeology. This is a far more powerful revealing because it is Nature's doing. The thousands of tonnes of sand and stone shifted by a single storm can be re-deposited by the next. The sea peels back 10,000 years, then puts it back. There is always excitement at the finds of human artefacts or footprints but for me it's the stumps themselves that matter – petrified, stripped of tissue, fungi and the other symbionts which gave the forest life – numinously revealed in the world. They are not metaphors or symbols but real things, once living now undead. These are woods at the edges of the world we inhabit today: real places, not imagined from what archaeology tells us. The space between the stumps may not be forest as we envision it, but it is still filled with an ungovernable wildness. The animals and plants have gone, what's left is the core essence of the trees. This could be more like looking into our future than our past; if anything could be seen, that is. We lean on the rail at the front. *Plick* says the sanderling unheard in the wind where the mad gull is motionless. We are looking out across waves chugging ashore. The forest is underwater, out there somewhere.

3.
STRAND

*Flotsam and jetsam washed up by the sea;
stranded at the very edge of the land in a temporary, tidal,
ridge-like line inhabited by living and dead things.*

MONSTROUS THING

Shadows drifted under clouds across Snowdonia and then vanished. Naked in the June sun on the hottest summer day for years, the mountains became ramparts as if they were the ruined walls of the world's end with nothing beyond. They made no reflection in the sea which was still and empty.

It began as a white dot drawing a line like a plane's vapour trail out of a purple streak of water at the far side of the bay. The white trail was the wake of a zodiac; its engine grew louder as it sped towards Criccieth and came to rest under cliffs below the castle rock. When the engine cut out there was a breathless tension over the sea. The driver made patting gestures with the flat of his hands to imitate the rapid slap of waves the other three passengers had just endured at high speed; a kind of signing as if not all of them spoke the same language. The four men looked similar: forties, large, muscular, ex-army. They spoke out of earshot without animation; concentrated, casual on their drifting inflatable boat, the understated formality of serious men who knew what they were about. They could not be followed or overheard. They were holding a secret meeting at sea: heist, assassination, coup d'état? Persons unknown, conspiring to commit a crime unknown. There were no witnesses, or so they thought. These were dangerous men.

Above the conspirators, derelict Criccieth Castle on top of its rock pushed against a perfect blue sky, stranded there by tides of history. Built by Llywelyn the Great, captured by Edward I, its stones had been raised by and dismantled by dangerous men of war, siege, bloodshed, politics. Now, in a faint breath of wind twitching dragon flags on top of the tower and floating a few gulls around, the castle stared blindly out to sea. Old and broken, the fortress needed a storm to restore the grand violences of its past when its engine tower catapulted rocks into the laps of its enemies. Instead the ruins found themselves interpreted as heritage with a visitor centre and gift shop for tourists and school parties, surrounded by a garden of pretty weeds.

A cinnabar took shelter from the sun in long grass: a black moth with scarlet dots and slashes, it settled in shadows. Out in the sunshine, pink thrift, white sea-campion and yellow cat's-ear flowered on cliffs below the castle walls. Fading three-cornered garlic and vivid fleabane bloomed where the cliffs joined a seawall below the promenade across the road from guest houses with vacancies, no vacancies. In that shingly cove under the castle, on the blind side of the rock from the men in the zodiac, a dead dogfish stiffened, eyeless in a patch of tangled fishing line, bright yellow horseshoe vetch and flies. The anglers in black packed up, lugged tackle back up the steps. The swimmer changed out of her wetsuit, driving off in a car advertising dancercise classes. The shore was empty but for a stray couple picking their way through the heat shimmer, a few oystercatchers abandoning the joy of panic to fold themselves in sleep and one or two of the lonely ones sunning on the wooden groynes. A serpentine sea, grey stones, black flies . . .

The cliff path headed west: past the limp good beach flag and gull-raided bins; beyond fields with sparrows, swallows, bees, buttercups; hedges of bramble, gorse and blackthorn where stonechats chipped like flints, pink balloons snagged on thorns and whitethroats sang above their hidden nests. Over the hot sand, a green tiger beetle flew, dropped to earth, ran, took off again until the path opened onto Ynysgain.

A tidal promontory of rock pools pointed seaward beyond a dark stone as big as a van on which cormorants perched like gargoyles on a tower, to an orange marker buoy in the water. High tide, low tide, spring, ebb and rakings in between, the strandlines like contours marked liminal altitudes. They stretched around the corner into the mouth of Afon Dwyfor. In the estuary a small flock of lesser black-backed gulls faced upstream, away from a black shed, the far castle on its rock and the high mountains behind. The gulls all faced into the marshes of Ty'n y Morla at the edge of maps.

On the Dwyfor estuary bend, before the ruined seawall, the strandlines twisted into one windrow of stuff: crispy pubic tangles of channelled wrack and kelp, mermaid's purses – black Bakelite egg cases of dogfish – white spongy bundles of skate eggs and lengths of blue rope. Barbed wire to keep cattle out of the river was hung with tatters of seaweed and bin-liners like rooks on a gibbet. The ground was covered in bits of plastic: drifts of it, mostly white, some linear, some circular; the identity of the products they came from lost to the pounding waves, fragmenting smaller and smaller pieces in the same process which manufactured the beach from shell and stone. This plastic had come down the

Dwyfor from farms and villages in the hills to join jetsam thrown overboard at sea and washed into the estuary.

Journeying plastic would find its way through the wild spaces beyond, grinding along the gyres of oceanic currents to gather in massive vortices, like those the size of Texas in the Pacific – Dead Star States spinning slowly with such gravitational force as to draw into themselves the world's disposed and dispossessed: beautiful detritus, chemical pollutants, millions of dead fish, turtles, dolphins and albatrosses – brown dwarfs waiting for Redemption Day when, as the Book of Revelation claims, the sea will give up its dead.

Something given up by the sea, hidden in swags of rope and kelp, was beyond redemption. Uncovered, it was like tarpaper studded with teeth. On one side the teeth were white, inch-long and plastic-like, knife-sharp, backward pointing fangs which drew blood instantly. Some were broken and some were just forming from the rough black skin. Closer inspection revealed the entire surface of the skin was made up of thorns, proto hook-teeth growing to replace the big ones when they broke. On the other side were skeletal remains: a fused spinal column, not bone but chitinous like dental plastic, with an elongated skull fragment holding what looked like eye sockets. Dark, dangerous, repulsive, it made no sense, the ruins of a being thrown up from the deep. This was a monstrous thing. Perhaps it was once part of a thorn ray, but it felt like the remains of some ghastly chimera – a sea monster made from fears and garbage. Unlike flotsam which floats and jetsam which is jettisoned, lagan is drowned cargo such as iron, timber, tyres, polyurethane, bone, fishing nets, stone and plastic bags sunk at the bottom of the sea. Treasure or trash, this stuff melded with creatures of the deep to form hybrid lagan monsters. Sometimes these things from dark unthinkable fathoms rose from the sea to haunt us.

A creature with a thousand writhing heads was washed up on a Cornish beach. Hurricane Katia had churned up a strange protoplasmic thing and dumped it on rocks at Crackington Haven. A thousand pearly white heads attached to a body of wriggling necks 40 feet long. They were goose barnacles, shells housing filter-feeding polyps on a 15-centimetre peduncle stalk colonising a tree trunk, thought to have originated from the Florida Everglades, dislodged from the seabed by the storm and after months tossed around, stranded on the far side of the Atlantic. The goose barnacles – so-called because in medieval times they were thought to be the eggs of barnacle geese, classified as 'fish' and therefore edible on a Friday – were still alive and desperate, scaring and fascinating onlookers.

The appearance of mutilated whales, seals, giant squid, fish, spores, plankton and algal blooms excited that mixture of fascination and fear which the American horror writer H.P. Lovecraft and others tapped into with tales of monstrous creatures, arcane legends and old gods imprisoned in the depths of the sea. Creatures seen at or around the surface have always been part of culture, from eighth-century St Brendan's Jasconye the Fish – the island that turned out to be a whale – to Melville's Moby Dick and the many imitations of the film *Jaws*; they are strange and, particularly in the case of sharks and jellyfish, dangerous. For many of us, the deep is an unknown wilderness, experienced vicariously through underwater documentary films from submersibles which travel to depths where the human body turns to mush. In these sunless, crushingly pressurised realms, live creatures that appear alien. They have evolved forms so unlike those ever experienced by landlubbers. And yet, there is something about recently discovered deep-sea creatures that evokes an ancient fear and awe, an emotion which survives from a very fundamental anxiety about wild Nature that has lurked under the surface of myths and legends about the sea.

The monstrous thing in the strandline was a relic of an unidentified marine animal broken from its original form and mangled into surreal juxtaposition with human debris. It awoke an unfamiliar confusion trying to identify it, a sinister fascination for the violence it was capable of with those teeth, a fear of its weird wildness and yet there it was surrounded by a homely sort of rubbish: bits of detergent containers, bottle tops and baler-twine. It hid at the boundary into our world like a curse. In Revelation 20:13 – 'And the sea gave up the dead which were in it'; this is also the title of a painting by Frederick Leighton (exhibited 1892).

The man in the bow of the zodiac gestured, describing some large space or thing. The others watched and listened intently; they had been in conversation for forty minutes before the driver started the outboard and the others positioned themselves for the high-speed return trip. The boat skimmed back the way it had come, its wake cutting across the lawless, secretive sea, rippling calmly as if it had no depth at all, under a cloudless, blank-blue sky, towards bare green mountains which appeared flat against the horizon, the space between filled with warm summer air glittering with intent. The zodiac took only a few minutes racing across the bay to Black Rock Sands where vehicles were waiting on the shore.

To the west, the monstrous thing, like some ancient munition activated by discovery and too dangerous to be left where it could blow up, was being buried under a stone. A shallow grave on the strandline for the unwanted gift from the sea, the dead returned long enough to bare its barbarous teeth, now safely tucked under the imprisoning weight of a gravestone. But for how long? To the east, four dangerous men went ashore to carry out their plan. Maybe whatever it was would make the headlines, maybe not.

RINGED PLOVER

The tide was coming in. Cwtiad Torchog is the Welsh name for ringed plover. He stood on the headstone of the monstrous thing. The ringed plover looked like a bird made from bits: sparrow-chested, gull-winged, spider-legged, bandit-faced, pencil-beaked. It had been pothering about the gentle spill of waves but a few inches high, its back to them, running before the edge, orange legs so fast: blur . . . stop . . . blur . . . stop, like a cartoon.

Furtive little thief: ringed plovers have in recent years taken to inland quarries and flooded gravel pits. They are not exclusively nautical, they're all about wherever the wet margin is; snatching worms, crustaceans and molluscs; the thrill of pick-pocketing the water's edge while it's moving. Ringed plovers hide in plain sight, out in the open stone and water ordered that Zen garden way – moving with the water's edge then still as stone – blur . . . stop – becoming each.

The bird picked through the meticulous chaos along the tideline, where small grey pebbles were rearranged, turned black and shining, by water; the sea's leavings washed into the gaps between them – tiny lives. Following the oscillations in and out, the plover continued its strand inspection, interrogating the debris: lines of seaweed, large plastic, small plastic, dead bodies of crabs and oystercatchers – watching, picking, running – blur . . . stop. And when a quicker, larger wave approached; when a shadow fell; when something moved, even a thought, into the running-watching space and spooked it, the plover's little back-pointed wings flicked it into the air. Then it became brown, buff, grey, black and white – the colours of Ynysgain, houses in the town, crags up the mountains, stones across the beach, ruins on the rock, clouds heaving over the horizon. And the bird flew quick and low over the sea's edge until it landed on that particular stone. There was a moment when the bird shimmered, even though it was still. And then it became invisibly still: a stone upon a stone. The tide moved up through gravel with a hiss as it aligned each bit of grit along its magnetic field. A wave licked down around the stone's edge to touch something buried there which had been dry for a long time, something that a dark reason must join to molecules from the depths beyond. When the wave touched, Cwtiad Torchog flew away. *Choo-ee, choo-ee!*

LION'S MANE

Like vomit, it floated nearer. A peachy-coloured wad, a wig, a tangle of fishing line, it rocked gently. All that mess was held in a clear bell, like plastic, tipped upside-down by the wake of a speeding boat. Unable to right itself, it pulsed faintly in the water, slowly shoreward. 'There is a wild spirit of good-naturedness which looks like malice,' wrote Friedrich Nietzsche in *Beyond Good and Evil* (1886).

This was a lion's mane jellyfish, palm-sized but too dangerous to handle. A big lion's mane can be ten times larger. The largest was reported from Massachusetts Bay in 1870. Its swimming bell was 7 feet in diameter and its tentacles trailed 120 feet. Further north, an Arctic lion's mane was found 8 feet wide with 150-foot tentacles, which made it bigger than a blue whale and therefore one of the largest animals on Earth. The largest was a bootlace worm, washed up on the shores of Scotland in 1862: 180 feet (55m) long.

Lion's mane or hair jellyfish do not just grow into huge individuals, they also produce huge blooms. Unlike the plastic Texases floating in the oceans, poisoning and smothering all life drawn into them, jelly blooms are floating festivals: within their venomous streamers, shrimp, medusafish, butterfish, harvestfish, young pollock and other symbionts find sanctuary. These blooms cause panic: threatening, deadly, invading hordes. One drifted into the headlines a couple of years ago off the Welsh coast. It was a swarm of millions covering 62 square miles (160 sq km). Experts put that down to climate change, warming seas, over-fishing and habitat destruction leading to a decline in predatory fish, seabirds and turtles. The jelly blooms were 'indicators of the state of our seas'. Marine conservationists warned lion's mane stings caused burns, muscular cramp, breathing and heart problems, even when washed up on the beach – even when effectively dead. The lion's mane – the collective noun for which is ironically a 'smack' – was a consequence of our ruthless exploitation of the marine environment; Nature's answering violence.

Because they don't swim but vaguely propel themselves by pulsing along ocean currents like wobbly hats, jellyfish are classified as plankton; they are the cnidarians. Within each lion's mane swimming bell, the gelatinous, pinky-orange body has eight lobes, each with a cluster of 60–130 tentacles barbed with nematocyte – a toxin causing paralysis. The oral arms around the mouth are for feeding on zooplankton, small fish, ctenophore – the beautiful comb-jellies that look like margin doodles – and they're also cannibals on other jellyfish species. In this 'medusa' stage, they have four ribbon gonads with intricately folded lips. Eggs are held by the oral tentacles and deposited on a reef where they're fertilised. The larvae, called planula, settle on the seabed and develop into polyps which form stacked discs like records on an old Dansette record player. The uppermost disc lifts off from the stack and drifts free to become the medusa and begin its travels at or near the surface.

What happens to the rest of the stack of polyp discs that don't take off? They became hostages from a more elemental time imprisoned in the depths while their chosen one hitched onto ocean currents to discover freedom in the Cnidarian Promised Land. It would never come back. This was a journey that began 600 million years ago. Genes found in jellyfish are nearly identical to those which switch on the bodybuilding processes for symmetrically shaped creatures, a process which caused the Cambrian explosion when the seas filled with new animal species. The nerve nets in jellyfish are the earliest examples of those same processes which form the human brain. This is the ancestor that created the fearful symmetry of the monstrous thing and the pathways through which travelled the dangerous synapses of the dangerous men. The lives this lion's-mane medusa left behind, way back in the Pre-Cambrian ocean, may one day become other species in a very different world.

Flipped by the surge from a powerful outboard carrying four men to their waiting vehicles on Black Rock Sands, the lion's mane jellyfish turned to the bright sky, stopped pulsing and gave itself up to landing. Alone and small, its poisonous tresses were snagged on sea anemones to be devoured. Its bell lodged in bladderwrack until a wave shook the wet laundry out and freed it to travel the last few yards. Laid on the strandline with wrack, gull-moult and polyurethane as waves sucked further out, the lion's mane melted into stones, a glistening smear leaving only its encrypted ransom note from the deep past. Cwtiad Torchog poked it with a stubby-pencil beak: the mark of destiny.

4.
RUIN

A destroyed or wrecked state; downfall or elimination;
the complete loss of property or position; remains
of something that has suffered ruin.

ROCK-LICKER

I lean against the gable end of a ruined cottage which rises
from rock under ash and sycamore trees. Its roof slope crests
with ivy, its whitewash stains with algae, its walls tumble
into ferns. There is a tiny window with the sliver of a frame,
not for viewing scenery but to watch for weather in the bay
and those passing on the lane. Now this hole lets in squalls,
and without its roof fifty winters have wrecked a house that
may have stood firm against three hundred more. I taste a
trickle of rain down the masonry, musty and sharp on my
tongue. I imagine I have business here.

A woman stares up at the towering keep of Ludlow
Castle and shouts disgustedly, *I've paid all this money to
come in and all there is . . . is ruins!* Unlike her, I have a thing
for ruins: craggy Marcher castles, grassy hill forts, derelict
iron foundries, de-sanctified churches, submerged villages,
empty pubs, vandalised telephone boxes, decommissioned
railway lines, overgrown gardens, burnt-out sheds. My
childhood is haunted by the ruins of houses, schools, sweet
shops and cinemas long abandoned and bulldozed. My
memories inhabit a landscape poignant with loss with no
evidence it ever existed. I love flowers in the ruins: Nature
reclaims our most audacious works and they disintegrate,
becoming colonised by plants and animals. I love the

romance of decay. Ruins have tearful edges, a melancholy which persists in places once cherished, alive, lived in, now desolate. Their stones, bricks, slates and concrete hold a recording of all that happened there and plays back to me like a distant gramophone. Ruins have a residual life absorbed by water and earth; they are a becoming. Rot is beautiful.

Wandering along the coast road between Dale and the field studies centre in the old fort above cliffs on St Ann's Head one October afternoon and seeing the ferny derelict, I feel the urge to call. With no dog to bark, no suspicious eye or challenge, I am an uninvited guest. I don't want to be a tourist. If I don't have a legitimate reason for being here, such as delivering the post, borrowing a drill, selling onions, I'd rather be a burglar. So I lean rudely against a wall I would not take such liberties with if the cottage were occupied and whole. I am not enquiring after the past of this place but of its future. This is what happens when we leave; when we up sticks and go away. This fate awaits those homes we love.

The transformation from home to derelict is not just about the absence of people. Without movement through the rooms the plaster pops and gravity takes over. Leaks in the roof become floods. Sly vandalisms of children become a demolition. This wreck is all that remains of a home whose occupants vanished into the memory of the place long ago. Driven out by poverty and hardship, they migrated to the mines of the Valleys or the factories of England or even further across the sea now glittering below the Pembrokeshire cliffs of west Wales. Down in the village, gulls call from the sea wall opposite a refurbished pub and the yacht club is closed on an October afternoon. The moorings are empty. Rooks clatter in treetops. Despite a lull in the wind and a brightness in the air, there is a haunting melancholy abroad. Autumn is the season of *hiraeth*. Literally translated from Welsh it is 'long field' – a poetic way of describing an emotion that exists in the land itself and winds into me from the walking of it. Meaning something more than 'homesickness'; more than a wistful longing for the old place; more than the legacy of diasporas exiled from these western lands of loss and lack; it is a mood which returns to a field filled with memories I never knew I had. Leaning here, I think they could be premonitions.

Unlike the shredding trees above and the exhausted-looking fields beyond them, the derelict cottage has a strangely luxurious green as if untouched by autumn's rot and rent. Ferns – hart's-tongue, smooth and flat as propellers; soft-shield, exotically filigreed; broad-buckler, branched little trees – grow with an intensity and relish out of wall stones and from under floorboards until only the gable stands above them. Too wet, too near the sea for frost, this is the Celtic rainforest: vegetation which survived the Ice Age and relishes the rain and the Gulf Stream warmth of the Atlantic seaboard, from Cornwall, through Wales, Ireland and Cumbria along the Scottish coast and Western Isles.

It is a rainforest in miniature and without flowers, growing on rocks, waterfalls, tree bark, ruins. Lean here much longer and I too will be greened over. Unlike flowering deciduous plants, shackled to the seasons and their shifting rhythms, ferns, mosses, liverworts and lichens have a far more constant, immutable green which is reclaiming the ruins to make a beautifully wild garden. Unlike the surrounding farmland, this green owes nothing to the history of people and belongs to an ancient world.

When the old red sandstone from which the cottage was built was laid down by sediments in another sea before the end of the Carboniferous era c.290 million years ago, the ancestors of these ferns were the forests of the world. Huge, majestic and flowerless, giant plants crashed to earth in unseen tropical storms and their rot became the stuff of power. Their fossils, buried under rock, blackened into coal, which, in the Industrial Revolution, changed the land and lives of this country. The coal-mining has gone now. Underground, the pits are flooded with memory, seams of labour and strife picked clean, mining communities betrayed and the ruins of their history darken in the space where coal came from. Carrying the ghosts of those gigantic Carboniferous forests in their cells, the ferns of the miniature rainforest inhabit a home abandoned by those who left to seek a better living from the coal.

A kestrel slides along the breeze over the headland to another ruin. This one, like the remains of a stone tower which once faced the sea, is all but smothered in bramble and ivy. The Pembrokeshire coast is littered with ruins. Even before Hubba the Viking found a safe haven here, the coves, bays and deep waterways held relics of marine conquest, settlement, commerce, fishing and industry. In Castle Bay are the remains of a kiln which burned lime to be sent by sea to furnaces down the coast. Lime was used as a flux to remove the impurities in smelting iron, up until the twentieth century. All that remains of that industry today is the derelict limekiln and a block of concrete in the beach holding iron mooring rings. I grip them and feel the creak of hawsers and the heft of lime boats straining on a tide long ebbed.

In the cove – half the size of the nearest supermarket – are strandlines left by tides, thick with loose oarweed – a brown kelp faded like strips of parcel tape – and purple laver – shiny as red cabbage, the seaweed eaten as traditional Welsh laver bread. The weed traps lengths of polypropylene rope, bright bits of plastic flotsam and other treasures from the sea. Within these tide-rows lives a colony of sandhoppers which explode in all directions when disturbed. Also stitched into the beach are rows of olive-brown bladderwrack and toffee-coloured channelled wrack with their holdfasts gripping stones under the sand. There is no one beachcombing except for a grey wagtail which, in a lemon flash, leaves picking through the strandlines and takes to a rock to flex anxiously above the slap of waves.

Here, between high and low tides, where the cliffs old red sandstone is scribbled with white lines of quartz polished by the waves, is a world inhabited by beautiful creatures surviving the crushing indifference of the sea. Unlike the sea potatoes, ragworms, peacock worms and lugworms, which bury themselves in the muddy gravels until snaffled up by curlews and godwits, the creatures of the rocky shore cannot disappear. Starfish like children's drawings endure the constant toilet-flush of rock pools. Sea anemones clench inside their own purple pillar-box bodies when exposed to air.

Loose on skimmer-stones of shingle are a few empty shells of *lampedu* which means rock-licker – the limpet. They are white, pearly, yellow-gold with coppery seams, conical, elliptical, translucent, ridged, not much wider than a 10p coin. These shells give nothing away about the creatures which made and inhabited them. The *Patellogastropoda*, true limpets, have a heart, a nervous system, kidneys, gills for breathing oxygen, a long gut with an anus twisted near the head which has two tentacles, each with a black eye-spot to 'see' light. The limpet is not entirely sedentary; it is a grazing animal which carries its stone tent on feeding expeditions, grazing algae growing on the rock with its rows of drill-bit teeth, moving by wave contractions of its foot-body which looks like a tongue – rock-licker. It has a homing instinct and will return from its pastoral journeys to the same 'home scar'.

Ground into the rock, this circular scar is evidence of the place where a limpet was set. The home scar reminds me of cup-and-ring marks made by pecking isolated outcrops, boulders, burial cairns and standing stones with a pointed rock. These pictographs appeared across northern Europe between 3800 BC and 1500 BC, from the late Neolithic to the Early Bronze Age. There are 5,000 of them scattered across Britain: enigmatic survivors of 'rock art', thought to be abstract marks with an unknown sacred meaning for their creators. The home scar is similarly the 'art' of the limpet, it's a public and private sign of personal territory to which it will return and resist being pushed out by others. The shell, which rises higher as the animal grows, will adapt to the contours of its home scar on the rock to make an exact fit. So powerfully does the limpet clamp down on its own place, sealing itself in against crashing waves and drying sunlight, it would rather be destroyed than let go.

When I count the annual rings on shells in Castle Bay like growth rings on a log, I see they survived ten winters, ten seasons of devastating storms. Yet for limpets, this is their season of sex. In southern Britain, rough seas from October to January trigger the release of eggs and sperm, as if they've been waiting for the most violent moment to ejaculate into the tempest. After fertilisation in the churning waves, the limpet larvae, which look like glass bulbs propelled by dancing waves of filaments, drift in the water column as plankton for a couple of weeks. All limpets are born male and, after finding their own place on the rocks, logs or jetty to stick to, the spat grow a shell and are sexually mature at nine months. After a couple of years they have a sex change. Most then become female, some stay male, until eaten by starfish, gulls, seals, people or until they finally succumb to the relentless pounding waves. In Castle Bay, seventeen-year-old limpets have been recorded – they go back to the Disaster.

At seven minutes past eight on the evening of Thursday 15 February 1996, a tanker called the *Sea Empress* heading towards Milford Haven hit rocks. Over several days, 72,000 tonnes of crude oil spilled into the sea. A filthy stinking slick filled these bays and 60 miles of coastline up to the high-tide mark. It was the largest and most environmentally damaging oil spill in European history. The news was full of the images of pathetic razorbills and guillemots – emblematic birds of the Pembrokeshire coast – doomed either by the oil or the detergent treatment to wash it off. I saw a small group of surviving guillemots, swimming in formation round and round a concrete pool at an animal rescue centre in Staffordshire, a long way from the sea. They had survived the oil and the detergent and were being kept in a cage until it was safe to return them. I wonder if they came back here or if the trauma finished them off. They were presented as symbols of hope but they were really tokens of reparation for a world ruined in the blink of an eye.

After the clean-up, beaches and coves took two years to recover their limpets. During that time, rocks in the bay were smothered by gut-weed, a grassy green seaweed released from the grazing pressure of the limpets, like scrub would cover the hills if sheep disappeared. Gradually, the limpets came back, licking the rocks clean on their secret journeys when no one was looking. Slipping their tongues over stone marbled like meat, dark, bloodily flesh-coloured and veined with white quartzite, the limpets kissed and licked it, taking in the gut-weed, removing the blemish. Driven by their own longing, the limpets left polished stone naked to the waves and returned to their love-bites until the sea proved too strong and they dropped, exhausted.

These empty shells in Castle Bay belonged to the first colonists following the *Sea Empress* disaster. High above the bay, at Watwick Point Beacon, jackdaws spiral around the 100-foot concrete tower whose beacon flashes a warning to shipping at the mouth of the Milford Haven waterway. As the light fades over this fjord of a flooded valley, one of the deepest in Europe, the prettily sinister white lights twinkle from its ports and refineries. Ferries with shamrocks on their funnels plough from Pembroke Dock to Ireland. Massive tankers slip in and out of the sea mist bringing crude oil from the Gulf States and liquid natural gas from Qatar, Algeria, Egypt, Trinidad and Malaysia to the refineries and pipelines at Milford Haven. A pall of black smoke, shaped like a tree, rises into the air above the refinery and drifts into the grey October sky. There is no knowing if this is a routine procedure or the prelude to another disaster. All this fossil fuel – made by animals and plants millions of years ago – travels around the world to be burned, creating a pollution which kills animals and plants of the future. This seems a particularly unintelligible kind of mystery.

'*Gwlad hud a lledrith*, land of mystery and magic,' is how the Mabinogion, a collection of medieval Welsh stories, refers to this part of west Wales. At the derelict cottage, no fire has been lit in the hearth, no smoke has gone up the chimney for a generation, maybe two. I listen as darkness settles under trees and the rooks and gulls return to their roosts.

Stories are told by firesides. With a clock ticking on the mantelpiece, flames rise from logs to lick the kettle boiling on a hook like the cauldron of Cerridwen, who emerges from Lake Tegid to brew, for a year and a day, just three drops of Awen – poetic inspiration. But the drops are stolen and the cauldron bursts and Cerridwen chases the thief in the form of different animals until she eats him, becomes pregnant and gives birth to a boy she throws into the river on 29 April. But on May Day the baby is rescued from a weir and begins to recite poems. He is Taliesin, bard of the Mabinogion and son of Cerridwen the enchantress, goddess of wisdom, rebirth, transformation and prophecy. Would that I was such a thief. The Neolithic dolmen with its ring marks on the hills above is called Womb of Cerridwen; it is where spirits of the dead dance.

Stories like this are told which may also have been heard by those who lived behind the clifftop earthworks or people long before them who were supposed to have shipped bluestone from the Preseli Mountains through here to Stonehenge. Histories of the people move through time like the breath of the sea. This cove is where Henry Tudor returned from exile in 1485; where land was owned by Rhys ap Thomas who claimed to have poleaxed Richard III at the Battle of Bosworth, and sent him to his grave under a car park in Leicester. Shakespeare called it 'blessed Milford Haven' in *Cymbeline*. Those lost at sea or gone to war or moved away; the disasters, scandals and gossip of generations retold as myth; the legends of people I knew too are a commonplace which becomes extraordinary in the telling: these stories rise like smoke up the chimney and drift across the night sky of *Gwlad hud a lledrith*.

I taste the sap of the Celtic rainforest on the ruined wall. Soon trees will push through floorboards and rubble and even the memory of this cottage and the lives of people who lived here will be a distant feeling, *hiraeth*. The small, overlooked things stick to the present with a kiss so passionate they leave a scar. Limpets on rocks in the bays below cast their genomes adrift in wild storms like *peregrini* – mad Welsh saints who threw themselves into the waves in shell-like coracles without power or navigation other than a fierce trust in divine destiny to find a rock to cling to and pray to enter the Kingdom of Heaven. The shells of beatific limpets on the beach are the ruins of a similar faith. Like them we evacuate our past, leave the land scarred by our love of it, and return to the elements. Yes, those shadows which haunt the 'long field' are not my memories, they are premonitions.

ETHER'S NILD

The neon needle of an azure damselfly snatches a spider from the daisy petals, rolls it into a ball and eats it as I watch, transfixed. Each of these lives, including mine, converges in one particular moment, beautiful and shot through with violence.

The colony of oxeye daisies is in full bloom and crackling with the static of insect life. Each flower has a golden-eyed disc of tiny yellow florets surrounded by the daisy ring of ray florets, the white petals plucked for divination: *she loves me, she loves me not.* This treasure attracts bees, hoverflies, beetles and true flies seeking pollen and nectar. Predators, such as spiders and damselflies come to prey on the pollinators and each other and I would be unwise to imagine myself exempt from this. Whatever forces are moving in, like the thunderclouds above hills on the western rim, may not invest my life and loves with any more significance than the spider's. What helps to resist pernicious feelings of doom or self-importance right now are the thunder daisies, moon daisies, dog daisies, oxeye daisies growing on the hedgebank. They grow around the remains of a brick stand for milk churns which were once collected by lorry every day at the end of the farm track. That hasn't happened for thirty years. There are few farms left with a small milking herd and although, to the casual eye, the countryside looks pretty much the same as it did when no one could have imagined an end to the ritual collection of the milk churns, it has changed immeasurably.

The churn stand has been liberated from its original purpose; it is now an ancient monument and appears to me as an altar. I stand before it as the Tarot magician: a fool leaving the cave into the land of milk and honey, into the light of understanding, thought and transcendence. But there's nothing there: just an old brick thing and a patch of weeds. I am a conjuror, an illusionist, a writer of stories. I wave my hand across the altar and a damselfly kills a spider in the daisies. Hundreds of milk-white flowers become a matter of life and death.

A grander illusion: the white flowering pulse of spring peaks with oxeye daisy. This wave of white wildflowers began on the turn from winter with snowdrops and went through spring with wood anemone, blackthorn, wild garlic, cow parsley and hawthorn, reaching its zenith in June with the oxeyes. Often seeded on roadside verges and becoming dominant from fertiliser enrichment, the daisies, with a passive, ox-like stare, watch the traffic, the insect dramas and the sultry drift from spring into midsummer. As the makings of another June storm gather, forming an oculus over the daisies growing on the hedgebank, the little bolt-of-blue-lightning damselfly zips off.

Its time is short. After a year as a nymph underwater, the azure damselfly only has a couple of weeks as an adult on the wing to do what 300 million years of dragonfly history has prepared it to do – secure the future. Modern descendants of bird-sized dragonflies in the fern forests of the Carboniferous, the small needling damselflies have an amphibious existence divided into two distinct phases: aquatic larvae – the nymph; and airborne adult – the damselfly. At least, that is the way we have been taught to think about them. Conventional wisdom dictates that although radically different in appearance, the larva and adult are but two stages in the metamorphosis of an insect that has a common ancestor and is only one animal. But what if the reason the two phases of metamorphosis look like two different animals is because they are? Then the insect is two different creatures, Jekyll and Hyde, a chimera, a monster.

Under the larval transfer hypothesis developed by Don Williamson, one of the most brilliant yet ignored British scientists of our time, one or more ancestors of the damselfly acquired the larva stage by hybridising with *thysanurans* – three-pronged bristletails. These are small wingless insects which move like fish, have small eyes, long antennae, ten-segmented abdomens and long *circi* – the three bristle-like sensory appendages – at the end. They like dark damp places and include silverfish, which scurry away when the light is turned on in the kitchen at night. Williamson suggests these *thysanuran* hybrids evolved into the nymph, the aquatic larva that still looks like a bristletail but with larger eyes, an expandable jaw for hunting water fleas and mosquito larvae underwater, and the circi bristles have become gills. The brown nymph moults its exoskeleton many times and before the final moult climbs out of the water up a flag iris leaf. It splits open. In the case of damselflies, there is less difference between the animals that have hybridised than between other insects such as beetles and butterflies and their grub or caterpillar larvae, so there is no need for pupation and the start-again metamorphoses where the creature must return to an alchemical broth of stem cells to magically reform into the 'adult'. Williamson says the Darwinian common ancestry theory has no explanation for the similarities between dragonfly nymph and *thysanurans*; it is not an example of convergent evolution, because the larva does not benefit from the resemblance, and 'nature would not select for it'. From the nymph, a goggle-eyed, trap-jawed, black and fluorescent blue creature with a ten-segmented needle abdomen loops out of its own skin. The veins of its gauzy wings, which come to rest at the sides of its body, not outstretched like dragonflies, expand and harden and it takes flight. It has become the azure damselfly and leaves the empty husk of a creature to which there is no return on the leaf – like a coat hanging on a nail in the derelict cottage. Former selves? They are not present in photographs; they cannot return our gaze or answer our questions.

The shape, colour and movement of damselflies gave them a reputation as stingers, even though they can't. No matter, they looked as if they could so were agents of the Devil and if people had known about their metamorphosis they may have been even more convinced of their diabolical nature. In her novel *Precious Bane*, Mary Webb, with an ear for the poetic in the country vernacular, used a Shropshire name for damselfly, *ether's nild:* the *ether* or adder's *nild* or needle because of its shape and stitching flight. Country lore had it that damselflies hovered over an adder coiled in the heath or bog as lookouts for their venomous master or mistress. Perhaps now the *ether's nild* hovers over the ether's ghost, the snake long since cleaved by a spade and hung on a fence as a warning to the others; the devilish not tolerated here. Elsewhere called the Devil's darning-needle, naughty children, scolding women and swearing men were warned that the damselfly would come and sew their eyes and mouths shut if they did not mend their ways. This is what happened to the Weald Moors: witnesses to the tragedy of this place cannot see or speak; they disappeared long ago, leaving few survivors and ruins. The *ether's nild* is also a compass needle, pointing towards the moors. I follow it.

I used to cycle out to the Weald Moors when I was a kid: to the cut, the canal at Wappenshall, to see damselflies and dragonflies; ride down the Duke's Drive, a long straight track across an expanse of flat fields and drainage ditches like the Fens of East Anglia; find little dark woods of alder trees, their great boles growing out of water and black mud. I still come here occasionally for the strange, wistful lostness of the place. Through the villages of Preston upon the Weald Moors and Kynnersley, I drove down the narrow bounce of Wall Lane to a pull-in by a gate. Gulls called over the low sweep of fields south towards the Wrekin hill and they were answered by coots in a pool and long puddles left by recent downpours. A flock of black Hebridean sheep were settled in a field. Beside the gate was an ancient alder tree, a relic of a much older land than the improved pastures surrounding; it stuck up there, rude and defiant with a gaping hollow, a living marker.

In the hedge opposite the alder tree, was a sign: an interpretation board with a painted illustration of Wall Camp. A mound rose from marsh and low woodland surrounded by a complex ring of earthen banks with moats of water between them. On the top of the mound stood a collection of thatched roundhouses, a few small fields or allotments and a fire whose smoke rose into a sky similar to this one, over two thousand years ago. The painting held a weird feeling of absence: except for the disproportionately large fire, there was no sign of life. It was as if a squatter settlement on the long deserted fort had just been evacuated as the result of some terrible event which was still burning there. Next to the sign were a small wooden fence and the gate. Beyond that, in the grassy field rose the ruins of earthworks with gorse bushes around the mound pictured in the painting. There were no signs denying or inviting entry, so I let myself into the field of black sheep then immediately through another gate into the field of Wall Camp.

The ground was wet; in the interpretation painting this would have been a wide ditch filled with water. I heard the sound of cattle behind me and turned to see a group of young bullocks crowded at the gate across the road from where I'd parked, pushing, shoving and yelling like a team of ginger boys. Then I noticed the rabbit. It was crouching oddly by the alder tree with a bundle of grass in its mouth. The rabbit ran up the lane, then reappeared in front of me in the Wall Camp field, cutting and stuffing more grass, probably for nursery bedding, into its mouth. Suddenly there was a noise above. I had been distracted by the bullocks and the rabbit and hadn't heard, until now, hooves pounding over the earthworks. First two russet-coloured cows and their calves charged down the bank at me. Then came the bull. They were moving very quickly. There was no time to run through the double gates to get out of the field, so I scrambled over the low wooden fence beside the sign. The cows came forward, tails up, turned before the fence and walked along the hedge. I saw the rabbit with its bedding bundle hide behind a hawthorn as the bull stopped about twenty paces away. Head lowered he pissed into the grass. He may not have been the biggest bull but he seemed massive to me. A head the size of a washing machine, huge neck and shoulders, long back, all deep russet red and rounded muscle – a brick shithouse of a beast. I looked into his eye.

This eye was unlike the oxeye daisy, which is really a pastoral joke in which the ox is prettified and conforms to a bovine ideal of cud-chewing reverie and disinterested stare. He was also not the snorting, charging, angry bull of cartoons. He was watching me closely with his robin redbreast-coloured eye, perhaps with a flash of gold in it. The eye lay at the forward edge of a body that could flatten a wall, not with a furious charge but with a mindful harnessing of colossal weight and strength of will. He was considering what to do. This bull was dangerous.

He began to eat, ripping up hanks of grass with his tongue whilst walking slowly but never diverting his eye from me. This grazing was subterfuge, getting me to think he was not charging while slyly gaining ground. I had heard of bulls working out how to kill someone and this felt premeditated. Perhaps it was payment for some mistreatment he had experienced; perhaps his hormones were pumped by the cows and his blood was up; perhaps something had woken inside that boulder of a skull, some wild bullness was taking over from thousands of years of domestication. It was going to be existential for both of us.

All that separated me from the bull was a rickety wooden fence 4 feet high. He could walk through it as if it didn't exist. I could turn and run. He was surprisingly quick for an animal that size and even if I got into the car he would be on me in seconds. He was practically as wide as the lane and I couldn't reverse out. The only thing to do was face him down. Stock still behind the little fence, I watched as he got closer and closer. Then his head went up and he gave a huge shake from his shoulders and his eyes boiled. I raised my right arm and waved him off, towards the camp. *Go on*, I said in as authoritative a voice as I could muster without sounding angry or afraid. The bull shook again and I repeated the gesture and the *Go on*. We were both still eye to eye. Then he stopped, half turned, so I repeated it matter-of-factly again. He turned around and walked back to the cows on the earthworks. My heart pounded.

The bullocks at the gate opposite had not been bellowing at me but alerting the bull, their father. I had trespassed on his land; my presence in his place was a threat to his herd and he had to meet it with that bull-thunder which rumbled between his scrotum and his head. But I had reasserted an ancient claim. The bull recognised it as the same claim the farmer used to assert his authority, the will to power which had shaped him and this land for millennia. I resented that but without the bull's compliance I may not have walked away.

The cattle sauntered out of sight into the Weald Moors, which here means *Wild Marshes*, a stretch of ancient marshland covering some 70 square kilometres north of Wellington, east of Shrewsbury and west of Newport. It is an out-of-the-way place, marginal, on the borders with

Staffordshire, the Shrewsbury Plain, part of the Severn catchment through the River Tern, on the outermost fringes of the Welsh Marches and within a triangle of three major Roman roads – little studied, unvisited. From the last Ice Age until it was finally drained by the Duke of Sutherland and the Commons Improvement Act of 1800, this was a series of fourteen linked moors: reed bed, fen, willow and alder carr, peatbog and grazing marsh, with island settlements within what archaeologists describe as a ritual landscape. Camps of Paleolithic nomads, scattered bits of Mesolithic stone tools, remains of ceremonial sweat lodges, Neolithic burning banks, Bronze Age round-barrow rings at river confluences, Iron Age fortified settlements, are evidence the Weald Moors had been lived and worshipped in for 10,000 years. On nearby Lilleshall Hill is a monument to the Duke of Sutherland: a stone obelisk donated by his grateful tenants, which stood as a one-fingered salute to the wild marshes. This was a landscape deliberately, painstakingly and intelligently ruined.

Most ancient marshes, fens and bogs in Britain were drained gradually since Saxon times but more rapidly and successfully by eighteenth- and nineteenth-century engineering geniuses inspired by the Dutch. During the last 300 years complex networks of drainage ditches, dykes, pumps and canalised rivers bled the Weald Moors, the East Anglia Fens, the Somerset Levels and created productive farmland and great wealth for those adventurers who invested in them. I imagined the marshlanders: a people apart, outlaws trying to resist Sutherland and the destruction of their world. I imagined an ancient ecology at the end of the Ice Age, before any drains were cut here: cranes and storks dancing, the boom of bitterns, the slap of beaver tails, marsh harriers haunting over reeds, diving ospreys, grazing elk and huge auroch bulls wallowing on a summer afternoon under a cloud of swallowtail butterflies and brilliant blue damselflies. All that wildlife and the legacy of ancient people gone down the drain; peat ploughed up and blown away; cultivated, civilised, sold. Only the damselflies remain.

Wall Camp is a hill fort without a hill. Shropshire is bristling with hill forts and one of its Iron Age capitals is on top of the Wrekin within sight to the south. Wall Camp is the third largest in the county, a fort built on an island in the marshes in the same fashion as a hill fort with rings of earthworks separated by wide ditches some archaeologists believe may have been a ritual maze; a rare survivor of prehistoric culture in the British Isles. The Weald Moors provided everything for its inhabitants: inexhaustible game, reeds, peat, even a salt spring. It had its own deities: the enchantress of watery places Cerridwen, shifted between creatures, boiled her cauldron of dark marsh pools for the drops of Anwen from which flowed a culture to be defended in encampments across the moors. My guess is the people who lived here three or four thousand years ago worked the Weald Moors marshlands like the ancient inhabitants of the Camargue river delta of southern France. Famous for its horses and cattle for centuries, the Camargue is also a place apart. How long the settlement at Wall Camp lasted is hard to tell. There are many abandoned settlements and deserted villages in Shropshire. Through the destruction of hill forts; crop failures, famines and plagues of the Middle Ages; evictions by the Knights Templar; theft of common land and enclosure by powerful landowners who even demolished villages to improve their view, many communities vanished, leaving only a few mounds in fields and, as in the case of Wall Camp, a single farmhouse. This land holds many ruins, each with its own lost history but in the Weald Moors, even the land is a ruin.

Along Wall Lane, with its oxeye daisies under dappled shade, I stood on Poor Piece Bridge. The stream below flowed like gravy through tangles of elder and dog rose climbing into ash trees. The stream was the Pipe Strine, one of a network of Strines – meaning small rivers (not Australian dialect) – including Strine Ditch, Red Strine, Strine Brook and River Strine which emerged from eskers – glacial sands and gravels – and had been engineered to drain the moors. The water, dirty with field run-off and its lost archive of boggy earth, formed part of the Severn catchment. In a patch of sunlight, a speckled wood and a peacock butterfly were knotted in aerial combat for a few seconds. Above them towered an old crack willow and a slight breeze through it caused a rippling of light on the lane. Formed originally, maybe five thousand years ago by layers of sticks and timber, this was one of the oldest extant ways in the land. And because the peat soils have wasted, drained, shrunk or blown away, the lane stood higher than the fields. Looking over a stile into another pasture of red cattle, the outer edges of Wall Camp's remaining earthworks dipped into the Pipe Strine.

Wild marshes were drained for agriculture, which became so intensive in the twentieth century it began to destroy itself. Now there were plans to restore areas of the Weald Moors to stop the water haemorrhaging and create habitat for wading birds on land where productive soils have been lost. The black Hebridean sheep were for conservation grazing and the flashes of undrained water were a hint at the future. Too late for reparation, such restoration may create a future wild marsh but the whole area is under pressure from water abstraction, soil wastage and development spilling from Telford. But what of the marshlanders who worked the Weald Moors for 10,000 years: outcast, vanquished and redundant; did they survive beyond wraiths of mist? Were they the nymphs who emerged from water to complete their monstrous destiny? In common with many abandoned settlements Wall Camp has been replaced by one farm and a very old name.

The name 'Wall' may refer to the ancient ruins or it may come from the words *volca* or *walha* used by Germanic tribes for foreigners, strangers and Romance speakers. Anglo-Saxons called the ancestral British population *wealas*. This Old English word did not just mean 'stranger', it described *the other*. The 'wall' in Cornwall and *welisc*, which became Wales, were lands of these 'other' people. Here, the names walha, wealas, wall, weald and wild are sewn together by the ether's nild, still darning holes in this worn-out place, stitching up the eyes and mouths of its ghosts.

CAILLEACH

It is one of the hottest summer days for many years and I'm leaning on a gate looking westwards, out across the wetlands of an island in the Inner Hebrides. Between low hills behind me and taller hills a couple of miles away, there's a wide shallow valley of wet grassland, fen and bog, divided by a grid of drainage ditches and narrow canal-like waterways. A track from the gate leads towards a small derelict house about a quarter of a mile away, though it's not marked on the map. There's no other sign of human habitation and the whole landscape is full of wildlife. A creaky sedge warbler sings from a gorse bush by the gatepost. Rising and falling into the wet flats are hundreds of birds: snipe, redshank and lapwing are piping, corncrake throw their rasping calls like ventriloquists hiding in nettle clumps and curlews flute and burble in the distance. All this sound is deadened by the fierce sunshine and hot, heavy air.

I let myself through the gate, onto the track, which is bordered at first with gorse bushes. These soon open out into a grassy mire with purple and pink flowers of northern marsh and heath spotted orchids, creaking with the sounds of crickets and slowly percolating water and flickering with marsh fritillary butterflies.

The track becomes spongier, wetter, with tussocks of grass and sedge and soon I'm hopping between them to keep out of the mud. There are deer slots and otter spraint but no human traces. Not a boot or tractor tyre has touched this track for years. My eyes are fixed to the ground. The birds don't seem too concerned by my presence but I'm careful in case there are still nests or chicks about. Everywhere I look there are plants and insects in the kind of profusion not seen in the rest of Britain for fifty years or more. This island really is a place apart.

On a raised, dry section of track I pause to look around. The feeling here is not what I expected looking out from the gate. Wild it may be but this is not wilderness and it owes its existence to a very human ambition. During the eighteenth century all this land was reclaimed from the sea by a Dutch engineer. What was once a tidal marsh between two sea lochs at either side of the island was separated by earth walls and drained to create fertile farmland for cereal crops and cattle grazing, all connected to the whisky distilleries. Because there's been no farming except some grazing for many years and because the drains have not been maintained, the landscape is returning to marsh again. This land should not be here at all.

As I flounder up the flooded track, I feel drawn to the house, the croft of those who farmed here. Apparently, some terrible tragedy happened in this house, but it's probably a story put about to keep people away. True or not, it certainly works: I've rarely seen a spookier place in broad daylight. A small flock of jackdaws and another of rock doves clatter out of the empty windows as I approach and curlews, clustered around the house, set up their cries.

As I get closer, there's a deep puddle which I edge around to the side of the house, into the remains of a garden with a circular stone construction which might have been a root store many years ago. It becomes suddenly cooler and quieter, a weird stillness. There are lots of bottles around, some of them sunk deep into the wet earth, untouched since they were lobbed there many years ago. From this side of the house, with rushes growing between stones and bottles, I look south along the sunlit wetlands but I'm aware of something cold and dark behind me, something ominous. I begin to hear a voice, faintly, threading through the curlew cries. It comes not from the land or from the house but from somewhere in between and in my imagination it's a young woman's lament.

I am a maid that's pined too long
For love has passed me by
Now bind my fate to a charm so strong
As to bring my sweetheart nigh.

When corpsies fly by the moon at night
And the hare runs through the heather
I shall prevail or die of fright
When I take the cailleach feather.

I watch swallows skimming over the landscape southwards, to where a huge bull I saw earlier at the side of the lane stands motionless, its coat the colour of winter bracken and its eyes shining like conkers. I'd stopped to see the bull before I pulled in at the gate here. He didn't seem to notice me and remained still; even when a cleg bit his shoulder there was barely a ripple through his flesh. The bull was staring across the bog at a tall narrow stone set on a low mound back from a fork in the road. The standing stone must have been there since the Bronze Age 5,000 years ago, and yet the bull stared at it as if it had just appeared. I wondered what that stone had been witness to for all those years: the weather of the seasons, the tides of migrating birds and all the countless generations of island people who had come to it – why, I can only guess. The bull stares at the monumental indifference of the stone; the two of them seem to symbolise the history of this landscape.

A wind begins to blow in from the north, there's a tang of salt in the air – a reminder that summer is short this far north and the swallows which are circling now above the standing stone will quite soon fling themselves off at a tangent south and the great skeins of geese will come in from the Arctic.

My true love sails from the northern land
As autumn leaves are falling
And I wait summer-long down on the strand
'Till I hear his voice a calling
He brings me a ruby he brings me a pearl
And shoes of finest leather
But I'm just a poor island girl
And I bring the cailleach feather.

I go to the front of the house. Grey rendering is peeling from the walls. Grass grows in the gutters. The front door is off its hinges blocking the entrance, so I peer through the empty frame of the window into what feels like impenetrable darkness. As my eyes get accustomed to the gloom, I scramble in through the window. The floor of the room is deep in dried cow muck. There are corpses of jackdaws and pigeons and the incessant buzz of flies. Even with the stink, the mess, the plaster hanging off the walls, this is a well-proportioned room, with an elegant iron range fireplace and a mantelpiece. It must have been a wonderful place to live: no electricity, no mains water, no telephone, yet a comfortable house in a beautiful landscape, living as close to the land as you can get.

I look out of the window. It's almost evening and the sky has clouded over. The gate seems a long way away. When I was walking towards it, the house felt sinister. Inside, it just feels old, vulnerable and sad. The more I look at the landscape outside the window, the more I feel it looking back at me. It must have been a tough life – growing turnips, rearing cattle, keeping the drains and waterways open – a constant struggle against the forces which were forever trying to reclaim the land which had been stolen from the marsh. Perhaps it was inevitable that the people would lose that struggle and the birds would win.

> With meadow flowers our garland winds
> On silver streams to flow
> With singing birds our handfast binds
> For only we shall know
> We make our vows beneath the stone
> He swears to forsake me never
> Our love shall live past flesh and bone
> Sworn on the cailleach feather.

This place is a kind of island in a sea of grass and reeds. It's the centre of a compass with hills to the east and west and the sea, north and south. Whichever direction I face, I am exposed to the elements and alone. The nearest town is 13 miles away, the nearest farm about 3 miles over the hill. The sense of isolation here is overwhelming. I wonder what its effect was on the people who lived here. Although the birds are singing and flowers are blooming, these long summer days are few and far between on the island. How did people here cope with being so remote, facing a landscape that would finally destroy them?

> The silkies moan through raging storm
> And gales howl round the chimney
> My true love's arms do keep me warm
> And the child that grows within me.
>
> A mother's prayer is for her waen
> Be fair, be proud, be clever
> A mother's heart will know of pain
> Touched by the cailleach feather.

This must be the room where they found his body. According to the story I heard, the old man who lived here would walk the 13 miles into town every week or so to collect unemployment benefit for himself and his sister. Then he'd maybe buy some groceries and spend the rest on drink. Many times he'd been found paralytic in a ditch on the way home. Having not seen him for several weeks, people at the post office asked someone who had to pass this way to check up on him. The old man was found in the armchair, boots still smouldering in the fireplace, his body half-eaten by rats, right here.

I walk to the back of the room, through a dark, derelict scullery into the other room at the front. This is where she was found. In this room the remains of his sister were discovered. She'd been dead much longer than he had, years maybe, and eaten by dogs.

> The land it yields but blood and stone
> There's shadows at our door
> My true love's thoughts return to home
> I fear he loves no more.
>
> Though grief assails us, I'll not weep
> Nor rest from our endeavour
> There's all eternity to sleep
> Hold true to the cailleach feather.

As I walk through the room I can see a gaping hole in the ceiling and stop to listen. *Hiss . . . hiss . . . sss*, it's the unmistakable sound of young barn owls, screech owls or, as they're called in the language of these islands, *cailleach*. In the Gaelic stories, the cailleach is the equivalent of the Welsh Cerridwen – an enchantress of pools and marshes, a giver of prophecy, who changes herself into an owl.

I don't want to disturb the owl chicks in the attic and the parent birds must be in there too, so I climb back out of the window. It's still warm but overcast and the light is fading. The marshy fields hum with insects and snipe drumming; the air rushing through their feathers as they dive earthwards from high up sounds like pantomime ghosts, *whooooo-oo*. I try to imagine what it's like in autumn and winter when the wild geese – the barnacle, bean, brent, white-fronts, pink-foots and greylags – come down from the Arctic in their tens of thousands to graze the marshy meadows and raise their broods here before they leave in spring. The wind shifts.

> My true love sails for the northern land
> At the blooming of the may
> And I leave my footprints in the sand
> For the waves to steal away.
>
> My sweetheart shall remember me
> At the turning of the weather
> When my soul will fly across the sea
> To avenge the cailleach feather.

I go round to the other side of the house. There's some slates missing from the roof right where I heard the barn owls. I'm listening to the birds as the first spots of rain begin to fall. Suddenly there's a flash of white and an owl slips silently from the house.

> When corpsies fly by the moon at night
> And the hare runs through the heather
> I haunt the dark and shun the light
> Cursed by the cailleach feather.

If the story I heard is true, no one has been to this derelict house for thirty years since the bodies of the old man and his sister were removed. Now only the owls live here and the bull shelters in winter. The marsh is reclaiming this slowly drowning land, sucking down the house into it like the old beer bottles. One day a storm tide will breach the sea walls and all this will return to how it was 300 years ago. How long will it be until no one speaks of what happened here, when only birds sing?

5.
FLOOD

An overflowing or influx of water beyond its normal confines; a torrent, deluge, river, stream, sea; the inflow of a tide influenced by lunar or solar attraction.

GREYLAG

'I was expecting the water to come in a wave down the street but it just rose out of the ground and flooded my house.' The young man stares into the camera in disbelief, his face already set telling a tale that will shape his future. In many years to come he will appear on television recounting the story of the day the floods began and he will wear the same expression as he recalls groundwater rising from the earth: inexorable, immutable, indifferent and beautiful. Under his feet, through sewers popping drain lids, through worm holes and the microscopic voids between sand grains, loam lumps; bleeding, blotting passages through soil and paving, wicking up footings and postholes to the light, the river infiltrates the land silently until – phenomenon of materialisation – the flood sheds its skin.

I watch the News with a mixture of sympathy for those affected by the floods and awe at the power of rivers. I watch the rains cleave along the watershed of Wenlock Edge. This way: south, down field drains, road gutters, ditches and prills into the River Corve. That way: north, down muddy woods, rutted tracks, field furrows, gippols under alders into Shienton Brook. Both ways lead to the Severn which now, without forced entry, burgles someone's living room in Tewkesbury, floats their coffee table like a little ark bearing the covenant of family photos, takes nothing but cancels everything out, leaving a scum-stain that never rubs off.

Floods may be temporary events but they establish their own reality, a natural part of the life cycle of rivers. The more we try to contain rivers by engineering them into ditches, ploughing up their catchments and building on their floodplains, the more devastating floods are when they happen. We turned away from rivers and behind our backs they changed. I want to counter the scare stories and hardening attitudes towards the wild life of floods because we have to find a way to live with them. But we do fear them and we should. Floods are happening more often. They will, because of climate change, alter how we use the land, dwell in it, imagine it. Rivers have woken in ways we are not prepared for.

This morning begins with the crackle of ice and a double rainbow. The Bifröst connects Earth to Asgard; the bridge between worlds; the symbol of the Great Flood. This refraction of light through raindrops twice, where the outer bow has the colours reversed, symbolises transformation. Given the epic weirdness of the weather and news reports from the floods, this rainbow seems doubly ominous.

It must appear so for the woman in the Somerset Levels who says, 'Last year we were told the floods were due to a once-in-a-hundred-years storm. This year we're flooded again, only worse.' It must be so for the villagers planning to ambush government ministers with DREDGE THE RIVERS banners spanning bridges; for Thames lock-keepers facing the overwhelming of their weirs, gates, sluices, warning boards and all the old rickety machinery of river management; for suburban householders in

Gloucestershire waking to find someone's nicked all their sandbags; for the Welsh coast publicans watching their roof flap through the sky like a wounded bird; for diners in a Cornish restaurant hiding under tables as waves heave boulders through the windows. Across the Bifröst steps an old god woken by new storms.

A strange thing heads towards Cressage bridge. Normally the River Severn swings from the south-west towards the Wrekin in the north then swerves south under the bridge at Cressage before bending south-east towards Leighton and the Ironbridge Gorge. Today, in flood, the river holds the whole valley and the road across the bridge is a tenuous causeway through a grey waterscape. There are powerful currents and eddies between lakes and the flood has its own being which has transformed the Severn corridor from the Welsh Hills to the Bristol Channel. Something catches my eye on the surface of the lake that was once fields. It's head-sized, rolling and bobbing awkwardly, knocking into fenceposts and hedgetops poking out of the water, past the near-submerged brick pillbox left from the war, gaining speed towards currents leading to the bridge. It twinkles. I lean against the bridge parapet to get a better look at the thing which rotates and sparkles even in such grey water under a grey sky. Suddenly it is spun by an eddy, grabbed by a muscly eel of current under the arch to be flung into willow branches, trapped for a moment on the other side of the bridge. It's a mirror ball. Spinning on the edge of roiling, roaring eddies under the stone arch, the mirror ball flashes to the music. The sound has a disturbing depth of pitch and a power which gives proximity to it, a feeling of both threat and excitement. This is picked up by a few blackbirds and great tits agitating in brambles under trees next to the bridge. Where did the mirror ball come from: the back room of a pub up in the hills, a swamped nightclub upstream? It struggles free of the willows, joins the flow around the bend, sparkles in its own wonderment, only a hundred leagues to the sea and the last dance ever.

Just a mile or so away, where the flood now covers ploughed-up water meadows, the mirror ball passed a place where swans and geese gather, an upping they perform every year. The swans are easy to see from the road. Sometimes there are hundreds of them on the fields, a striking white-on-green heraldry. The geese are less noticeable, grey like river mud from a distance, full of the flow of colours between sky and water close to. The waterfowl have gathered on the flood meadows, now used for arable crops, to graze in community during the winter months before dispersing for the breeding season. The flood may have taken much of the grazing land away from them but it has given the birds a renewed grace that fits the flow of wild riverlands.

Before drains and embankments and ploughs, the Severn was a many-channelled braid of flows and expansive in its flood. The birds were here then as they are now, drifting on shelves of water at the margins, standing watch, honking through the sky on wings they love the sound of, slapping their own reflections off the surface as they plane in out of nowhere. They belong to the River Severn's floodscape and they are part of a mystery of birds and water that travels way back into our culture, certainly to the origins of English.

This is a thousand-year-old riddle: *Silence is what I wear when I walk the earth or make my home or stir the waters. Sometimes my beauty and these high air currents take me*

above the houses and the power of clouds lifts me over nations.
My charms resonate strongly with melody, singing when I am
away from the flood or the earth – a travelling spirit.

Who am I? Silence, water, flight, beauty, music, travel
– long before the Norman Conquest, an English writer
posed this riddle about the mute swan. This is a translation
from Old English into Modern English and the swan,
moved by the power of clouds and its own magic, is lifted
through a thousand years of the same language. People we
call the Anglo-Saxons brought this language from the river
valleys, fens and estuaries of northern Europe. They came
to Britain with swan symbols on their sword handles and
swan maidens dancing through their creation myths and
they built the water meadows. Our language and waterfowl
were wrung from the same floods.

We can feel the truth of this on winter mornings, when
the sun arcs low above lead-grey water and glints on the
white plumage of swans as they slide out of the mist.
Silently gliding or wing-smacking the water, our language
struggles to keep up with swans. And the riddle? A question
to confuse and then reveal like a conjuror's trick: the swan
flying into the heart of our culture, linking our lakes and
rivers to the ancestral north across the sea – which the
author of *Beowulf*, the first great poem in English, called:
the *swan's road* and sometimes the *goose road*. Swans and
geese are often interchangeable in the language of legends,
part of a lexicon of birds and trees that carry meaning
between culture and Nature. I look along the flood's edge to
see gaggles and skeins: flying, landing, standing, waddling,
flapping, feeding, arranged like words in sentences, stanzas
– poems of birds.

These mute swans and greylag geese on the Severn above Cressage bridge may not be the ones that come barrelling down the swan roads from Siberia or Iceland. They may be hefted to these riverlands, descendants of royal birds or ancestors of domestic geese whose wings were clipped, whose big webbed feet were made to waddle through tar to harden for long droves to goose fairs. Either way, they are creatures of the flood now. Flood in its old poetic sense held a glossary of names, largely replaced in modern English with the managerial term *wetland*, a sump where the poetry of water drains. As the flood reclaims its lands, so language can reclaim its names: burbling with brook, beck, burn, bourne, stream, prill; arterial with rivulet, river, afon, meander, canal, waterway; dramatic with floods, flashes, washes, was, deluges, soddenings; upwelling with oozes, seeps, flushes, springs, wells, fonts, founts; sublime with falls, cascades, torrents, pystill, spouts; rude with ditches, drains, dykes, flushes, channels, scrapes, cuts; glittering with lakes, llyn, lochs, meres, fens, broads; intimate with puddles, ponds, pools, tarns, cymau, corries, pingos, flarks; dangerous with swamps, sloughs, quagmires, swingsholms, marshes, mosses, bogs. All those trickles through soil into dark underground cave systems and aquifers and eventually out to the saltings, mudflats, sandbars, foreshores, estuaries, rheas, fjords, deltas. Where are all those soggy bottoms and damp patches I can't remember? We owe it to all their sopping, sloppy, soaked, sodden, muddy, mucky, mired, wringing wet and unreconstructed *wild* lives to celebrate them by their proper names.

Across the Bifröst goosesteps the greylag; she shakes thunder from her wings and wipes her beak in the water, the world bigger, more wondrous and hers again.

HERON

It was August bank holiday and I watched a heron stalking the shore like a knife on stilts. There must have been hundreds of people enjoying the sunshine: walking, picnicking, boating, throwing sticks for dogs, skimming stones on Lake Vyrnwy in mid-Wales. They all seemed oblivious to the heron haunting the lake's edge, flying over the glittering water surrounded by the Berwyn mountains. Buzzards spiralled slowly on thermal currents through a clear blue sky and I imagined fish deep beneath the cinematically reflective surface of the lake, following their own currents underwater. It was a day of intimate moments in a sublime landscape but I had a bad feeling about it and the presence of the heron was ominous.

Ovid said grey herons rose from the ashes of the destroyed Roman city of Ardea. Their Latin name is *Ardea cinerea*, grey. Celts – for whom these birds were spirits doing penance – connected herons with divination and mystery. I have always felt herons to be beautiful, fascinating but ominous birds. The direction of their slow, solemn flight on wide wings, legs swept back, neck folded and spear-beaked head pointing like a compass needle always feels significant and their priestly – to use a Dylan Thomas image – movements at water's edge appear ceremonial. As it vanished from sight, only the heron's savage *kaark* was evidence that it ever existed. It left me with an unnerving sense of loss as I wondered if this augury of a bird was searching for something here, another lost Ardea, because, in an odd kind of way, that's why I had come to Lake Vyrnwy.

I am fascinated by the idea that some places frighten us for reasons we don't understand; places that feel weird, eerie, sinister, the eldritch places from the Old English for a strange country, the Otherworld. Many people have the feeling they are being watched or there is something spooky about a place which makes them want to get out of it. I have had several very strong reactions to places in woods and on mountains where I've felt uneasy, as if something has happened there which has been so powerful because of its violence or sadness that it has left an imprint in the trees, rocks, earth or walls of the place itself. Everyone I talk to about this has a similar experience, which ranges from a place not feeling right to a real dread or terror of somewhere for no particular reason.

The eldritch feeling I had at Lake Vyrnwy was called Llanwddyn. This was the name of the village flooded in the nineteenth century during the construction of the Lake Vyrnwy reservoir needed to supply fresh water to Liverpool. One summer in the 1970s there was such a drought that the water level in the reservoir dropped to reveal buildings and streets. Like many other people, I came to gawp at the ghost village lost underwater for the last eighty years. It was weird and spooky all right, but it had such a profoundly disturbing effect on me that I scarpered and never went back, until now. I've come to face that feeling and try to understand what it meant. The poet R.S. Thomas hated these reservoirs in Wales. He refused to visit them and was revolted by the apparent serenity of the lakes which he said concealed the subconscious of a drowned people.

The subconscious is a weird place, an underworld of secrets, sinisterly reaching beyond the 'people far down' into our, your, my subconscious. When they flooded Llanwddyn in 1888, the Liverpool Corporation built another village with the same name for the people to move into. It has reinvented itself: a thriving community with a parish newsletter sporting an ironic picture of a village under-water. Those who were evacuated left behind a post office, the parish church, 2 chapels, 3 pubs, 37 houses, 10 farms . . . glug, glug, glug. The big Gothic dam stopped the river and drowned the village: where the dead had to be shifted out of the graveyards, where there was nothing to drink but water in the Cross Guns; all those years scrubbing the front step, now it was eels up the chimney and pike with terrible teeth cruising the old gardens of roses and runner beans. And what else drowned down there? A village is not just bricks and streets and gossip. A rare cluster of archaeological remains – barrows and burial mounds – show the Vyrnwy valley was a place sacred to the ancient dead for 5,000 years.

When the day-trippers drove back to the West Midlands or Merseyside and the sun began to set on the August bank holiday, I found myself wandering the shores of the lake. Standing on mossy boulders below Rhiwargor waterfall near the stream's mouth in the fading light I could just see the shapes of bats flitting over the still waters then zipping under trees overhanging the stream and swerving past my head before looping back out across the lake again. There were perhaps hundreds of them hunting the kind of flies anglers imitate to catch trout, just above the water's surface. It struck me that I could hear the thrum of their wings and maybe some faint sounds but I could not, even with the equipment that draws down their frequency to something audible to me, hear what bats hear. Echoes bouncing back from the ultrasonic clicks and squeaks of bats defined their world. It would sound exciting, manic, a frenzy of feeding but so ordered that each bat avoided collision and drowning and each was aware of the others. This darkness was illuminated by bat voices and senses of perception I could only guess at. And what was I to the bats, moving slowly and standing in the stream under a darkening sky? I stood entranced, bats swooping through their songs all around me, appearing to fly out of the lake and into my imagination.

A congregation filing through the streets like dippers walking under the river, sings at a funeral in old Llanwyddn; sings like the eerie laugh of black grouse in the rain on the Berwyns; like water from a tap in the toilets of a pub in Liverpool; like the heartbeat of Lime Street and, from the stream of Rhiwargor, voices of the Old Ones flying from the lake.

I watched a heron fly across the implacable surface of Lake Vyrnwy. I had not come here for the watercolour scenery but to confront what R.S. Thomas called the 'poem's harsher conditions' and pay my respects. There must have been hundreds of people enjoying the sunshine, walking, picnicking, boating, throwing sticks for dogs, skimming stones. Everyone seemed oblivious to the heron haunting the lake's edge and then, *kraak*, flying slowly over the glittering water.

WATER BOATMAN

In County Kildare in Ireland, below the Point of Gibraltar in Pollardstown Fen, where the north and east drains joined, the boatman's world would open down the Milltown Feeder to the Grand Canal and Dublin, then to anywhere in the whole wide world across the sea. And so, leaving his true love at the fen's edge with only a promise they would marry on his return, the boatman rowed away across the cool clear water to find his fortune. Now he was back to claim his bride but she was gone, betrothed to another and the fortune he found meant nothing to the love he'd lost. The boatman threw a rope over an arch between the canal and the road down to the Curragh. His tears fell, to be carried by strange creatures of the water, back beyond the Point of Gibraltar where the drains married, into that wild place, Pollardstown Fen. The boatman's song lives there still: the lost love of a Hanged Man.

There he is in the Tarot cards, upside-down for sacrifice, death and regeneration, the end of one thing and the beginning of another. And he turns up in *The Waste Land*, as T.S. Eliot says:

> I do not find
> The Hanged Man. Fear death by water.
> I see crowds of people, walking round in a ring.

But no, listen, not people – crowds of stranger creatures, water boatmen – seed-hard little insects swimming upside-down, carrying a tear of air, rowing with their oar legs through the cool clear water, their songs rippling round the Hanged Man.

'The wrong one was hanged!' said the landlord of the Hanged Man's pub, telling the boatman's tale. So who should have been hanged instead: the faithless girl? She who was abandoned to live on promises and hide like a vixen in the reeds until her roving boy returned; she, the lost love, still haunts the fen. But what about the men who dug the drains and broke open the fen to the world; what about those who would steal the water from its sacred springs, tame its wild places and purge its creatures – don't they deserve hanging? My guess is, the Hanged Man's landlord is telling a new story now, about three men in a boat wobbling into the fen to do some story for the wireless. And if it looked so funny, and it did, that would be Jim's fault.

Tom and I are watching the clear flow of a canal, the Milltown Feeder, across the bridge from the pub built where the boatman hanged himself. Tom Lawrence is a musician, composer and acoustic ecologist and I've come to Ireland to research a script for a radio programme about him and the place where he records underwater sounds. Tom says, jokingly, 'Well, I suppose you've met another sound recordist called Tom who disappears?' A year or so earlier I had written and narrated a docudrama for BBC Radio 4 called *The Ditch*. This was a fictional story about a wildlife sound-recordist called Tom Saunders who goes missing on the East Anglian coast. I had been doing field research for the story in Suffolk and Norfolk where there are still places on the English coast remote and bleak enough to have preserved their wild character through the ages. In my play, Tom Saunders found such a place, Slaughton Ditch, a maze of muddy creeks and shingle banks in East Anglia, and fell in love with it. As a respected if maverick sound recordist, Saunders built his reputation on capturing high-quality wildlife and landscape sounds for radio, television and film. Slaughton Ditch is where he'd done his best work and he and the narrator were planning a natural history radio documentary about the place when Tom went missing. It was assumed Saunders had an accident and his body had been swept out to sea. But when the narrator received a package from Tom's solicitor containing a collection of sound recordings and a notebook, he began to suspect the story wasn't that simple. Ploughing through Saunders's crazy ramblings about EVP – electronic voice phenomenon – and the weird recordings he claimed were voices of malevolent intent from the past preying on the living, the narrator went out to Slaughton Ditch to try to find out what happened.

What he discovered was evidence of Saunders's obsession with some wild power that lay within the sounds of this beautiful yet sinister landscape. The narrator became aware that he had been deliberately lured to this place to tell a story and complete the documentary they were working on. Did Saunders get the narrator to record what he believed was his own EVP as a desperate attempt to belong here and achieve some kind of immortality? Was this all an elaborate hoax, a tragic accident or had Saunders stumbled on a hidden but terrifying truth? Although uncertainty surrounds Saunders's motivation and fate, what the narrator experiences through his quest for the truth is both haunting and terrifying. The brilliant Chris Watson recorded sounds for *The Ditch* and Tom Lawrence tells me he is very taken with it and the whole eco-gothic idea I'm trying to develop.

The day is a bit flat and cloudy, the forecast speaks of rain; it is quiet but for traffic bouncing over the canal bridge and a big brown trout slaps the water. But it is what's going on below the surface of the water that's brought me across the Irish Sea to a remote fen. Down there, in Pollardstown Fen, is a world that Tom has spent a year recording. From a couple of telephone conversations, some messages and a flurry of emails, I know Tom's enthusiasm to be infectious. I'm intrigued. Tom claims that aquatic insects I have given little thought to since my pond-dipping childhood are sources of a secret, strange and violently exciting kind of musicality. He has prepared me to be impressed but nothing could have prepared me for the singing of water boatmen.

Tom has agreed to take me into Pollardstown Fen and show me the places where he recorded. The last time he was in the Hanged Man pub he met photographer and outdoorsman Jim Schofield, who said he could bring a boat and take us into the heart of the fen, no problem. That's what we're waiting for. But when Jim pulls in he isn't towing a boat or anything. We chat, he puts on a wetsuit and like a magician pulling a rabbit out of a hat, he opens the boot of his car and drags out what looks like a shopping bag, inside which is an inflatable boat. This is a boat without ego, without shame – more like a child's blow-up paddling pool powered by a food mixer – and yet it turns out to be exactly the right kind of craft for these waters. First the demented ho-down, stomping life into the inflatable through a foot pump, then the undignified wobble up the Milltown Feeder into a different world.

A canal mile on the water is a measure of time as well as space: slower, longer, floatier. It could feel interminable with two other blokes in this plastic bathtub but it's a joy. Jim is wiry with a brush beard and brimming with restless energy; Tom is quieter, with deep reserves of wit and intelligence; I feel like ballast but am aware this trip is for my benefit, and

I don't know what to expect. We swap stories but become more rapt in the landscape the deeper we get into it. Away from the roads, buildings and communication signals, this is a different Ireland. Our moody little motor putters along a 10-metre-wide canal and, despite Jim's assertion that our lifejacket's only function is to make our bodies easier to find, it's only a couple of metres deep. The water level is, however, higher than the low-lying fields and hedges of County Kildare and we have sweeping buzzard-like views to the faraway Wicklow Mountains. This landscape is the deep green survivor of war and famine and yet it is sinking as the peat soils shrink; draining, flowing away.

There was much more of it here in the 1870s when the poet Gerard Manley Hopkins would escape from Dublin, where he was going out of his mind, to this watery landscape and breathe its 'delicious bog air'. Hopkins found renewal and creativity in Nature here, just as Tom Lawrence has and I imagine him drinking it all in and feeling this wonderfully fluid sense of space, as I am too. Just as I think this, the view begins to close in under fringes of tall reeds, a tawny palisade of stems, green leaves and conspiratorial whispers. This road of clear water through patterns of light leads into Old Ireland.

Pollardstown Fen is a 12,000-year-old relic of an Ice Age lake and one of the last remaining alkaline, spring-fed valley fens in Europe. Forty springs bubble through thick grey marl to keep this world afloat. The springs come from under the Curragh, a 5,000-acre plain of glacial outwash sand, dedicated for centuries to galloping horses. My grandfather Eric came here for cavalry training in the Great War; a lad from a Shropshire farm with his own horse, also called Tom. Pushing up through the Curragh's northern edge, these springs are the mythically replenishing force: the fairy cow that won't be milked dry; the full glass that can't be emptied; the sacred dripping tap. Only 550 acres of Pollardstown Fen survive drainage, peat-digging and fire damage and now it's all protected by law to save the unique community of wild lives it holds. Tom knows the law alone will not protect this place and he has become a passionate advocate.

As sentinel to this waterland, the darkly craggy ash tree at the Point of Gibraltar seems to stand for a more ancient law and the canal ends at a fork in front of it. In the 1790s two deep drains were dug into Pollardstown Fen to supply water to be carried by the Milltown Feeder canal feeding the Grand Canal into Dublin. The water feels so vibrant it's not surprising to learn it was once the main water supply for the Guinness brewery. We take the left fork, North Drain. The tiny propeller fouls on a mattress of floating pondweed. The following stillness is not silence but the absence of noise; surrounded now by the scratchy little tunes of sedge warblers in the rustling reeds, we feel the slight heft of water and something beyond our hearing.

Ducking under willow branches, my paddle turns up the unmistakable form of a dead snake. We fish it out: the first snake found in Ireland, the one that escaped St Patrick's banishment? Jim grabs it and pulls. Rubber.

We are heading towards Seven Springs, deep in the fen at the end of the drain and the source of its crystal water. There are white snail shells on the peat bed below and white clouds coiled in the sky above. There are skimming swallows and lurking swans and grasshopper warblers reeling out their songs from hiding places in the reeds. We haul up a drowned holdall from an underwater garden of whorled water milfoil bubbling with oxygen. Is it a bag full of the hanged boatman's fortune? Empty beer cans.

I worry that Tom's patience is straining as his mission to get me to the places he's recorded gets tangled in blokeish banter. He wants me to feel the specialness of this place in order to understand his recordings. As we fool about enjoying the craic, water beetles and water boatmen go about their watery business. I watch these insects swimming, hunting and searching for mates or whatever they're doing and as fascinating as they are to me, they seem no more extraordinary than the brilliant dragonflies and butterflies flying through the still fen air. However, Tom's revelatory recordings show the aquatic insect phenomenon is far more wondrous than that, or finding a bag of treasure or a mythical snake.

It was a calm still summer day like this when Tom first dipped a hydrophone – an underwater microphone – into Pollardstown Fen. What happened was life-changing. He heard such a terrible noise he thought his kit was broken. After checking for gremlins in plugs and cables and testing everything he could to satisfy himself there was nothing wrong with his recording equipment, he tried again – same thing: a screaming banshee wail made him aware it was the human ear not electronic gear that couldn't take it in. Tom's hydrophone was picking up the warning cry of a water scorpion – dark predatory Scorpio, a water sign, chasing Orion through the Cosmos, ruled by warlike Mars; not really a scorpion but a bug only 30 millimetres long. Shocked but fascinated, Tom began to record aquatic insects as scientifically as he could.

Tapping, knocking, hammering, drumming, clicking, creaking, cracking, croaking, buzzing, fuzzing, bleeping, winding, reeling, revving, puttering, pattering, humming, pulsing, squealing, shrieking . . . the insects reveal themselves. They are whirligigs, water beetles, great diving beetles, water boatmen, lesser water boatmen, a hundred species of creatures which can keep these extraordinary sounds up all day, at over 2kHz, reaching 99 decibels – the equivalent of hearing a full orchestra from the front row. They are singing, like birds, to attract a mate, to warn off rivals, to stake a claim. They are communicating, as we do, their moving, breathing, feeding, sexual frequency in the world.

For centuries we've known grasshoppers rub a row of pegs on their hind legs against thickened forewings and crickets rub their wings together to create those fiddling tunes so evocative of summer; this is called stridulating. Only fairly recently it was discovered that aquatic insects communicate by stridulating, too. Using specially adapted structures on their limbs, heads, wing cases and, according to recent research on some species of water boatmen, their penises – the stridulatory pegs are rubbed over a plectrum to cause a pulse of sonic vibrations which can increase in intensity. The more pegs scraped over the plectrum, the more variable the pitch, intensity and rhythm of the train of sound.

Under our daft boat, under the threshold of our hearing, under the surface of the water and its symbolic function as the skin of our reality, lies another Ireland – a country dominated by insects here for 12,000 years. It is really humbling to hear sounds that emerged many millions of years ago, and what power they have! I put the headphones on. I see the grin of triumph and recognition spread across Tom's face when he knows I'm listening to the sounds of water boatmen. I am perplexed and entranced. Sounds I've only ever heard in avant-garde electronic music are being made by a bug the size of a pip. It's like listening to an alien intelligence, both violent and moving. If Tom were to tell me this is the origin of music, that our own music was only an adaption of what the water boatmen were 'singing', I'd believe him.

Each water boatman carries a bubble of air held tight to the body, replenished by frequent upside-down visits to the water's surface and from which it absorbs oxygen through tiny holes in its exoskeleton. These air bubbles also act as receivers for vibrations of sound produced by other stridulating insects. At certain frequencies, sound received by the air bubble stimulates the bubble's carrier to stridulate as well. This stimulation seems to cross barriers of species and, like a song, it passes between individuals of the aquatic community. I think of the air bubbles as tears of the hanged boatman, carrying his song through the fen.

We paddle around on the ceiling of this extraordinary sound garden, getting plugged by water mint and stitched into smaller puddles by reeds and willows until the only way to go is the way we came. Half reluctantly we make the return journey, trailing behind swans which spank the water hard and in so doing restore the reality we come back to.

When we get there, we find we don't quite fit in any more. We appear so comic to the landlord of the Hanged Man's pub he must think the fen spat out three clowns on a lilo. After a drink we feel more rehabilitated but I need to get my bearings, to see Pollardstown Fen in its own landscape; so we head off to the Hill of Allen.

The steep woods let out onto a strange hilltop, 600 feet above sea level, scorched and enclosed by chain-link fencing. Here, on the ancient royal seat of the legendary Finn Mac Cumhail, rising 60 feet above the pit where bones of the giant warrior were found, is the tower. Known as Aylmer's Folly, it was built on the Hill of Allen by Sir Gerald Aylmer in 1859. Some say it's a famine tower: a job creation scheme providing employment during those terrible times. Tom wangles a key from the quarry company which owns the hill; we go inside and climb the eighty-three steps, each with the name of someone who helped with the tower's construction cut into the stone. The tower is fascinating and troubling, too. It's a folly but it's also a kind of divining rod stuck between the rock and the sky; its narrow spiral staircase to the lookout has a resonance hard to describe.

Tom wants to show me the view so that I understand where I've been more clearly, not as a tourist but as a participant. Tom is rigorous. Phew. Right at the top is a kind of conservatory and we squeeze through a window like inept burglars, out onto narrow battlements and the swirling vertigo of Leinster. As I try to collect my senses, a dark shape speeds through them like a spinning knife. A peregrine falcon flies from clouds as tall and grey as the quarry in the hill below; homing in from the far Wicklow and Slieve Bloom Mountains, over the long flat miles of the Bog of Allen being opencast mined for peat where, as Seamus Heaney wrote, every layer of peat stripped away held evidence of being 'camped on', inhabited for millennia.

Here's a land blasted by progress and blighted by the need to make it pay. There, a rude wild relict place in this scraped-clean landscape is Pollardstown Fen, where Heaney might claim, 'The wet centre is bottomless.'

The peregrine's call rings from the quarry below: a harsh, strident, predatory sound on the same savage frequency as the insects underwater. We climb down from the sky and leave the Hill of Allen to falcons and feral youths, inheritors of Finn Mac Cumhail's Fianna.

Jim Schofield drives home, with his boat-in-a-bag and swans in his camera. Tom Lawrence and I go back to Pollardstown Fen. We enter by the front gate as it were, into the car park where Tom recorded joyriders' screaming rubber doughnuts. Here, the interpretation boards and all-weather paths seem to fix the place to the world of surrounding motorways and military noise, towns and troubles of our times, instead of freeing it to be its unique timeless self.

Tom demonstrates his recording technique by lobbing a hydrophone into the water with angling proficiency and passes me the headphones. I listen. *Bang . . . bang . . . bang . . .* it's the anvil-hammer beat of a great diving beetle, a creature as predatory as a peregrine falcon and every bit as dangerous and confident in its environment, a thrilling sound.

Thud and shudder, the peat under the boardwalk bounces with footsteps. I feel. People come for their evening constitutionals with kids and dogs on the loose; birds challenge them from the willow scrub; Tom eyes them sideways, he's suspicious of those who appear to lack respect for this place. Off piste, the fen grasses with their own green fluidity hold orchid treasures. I look. Now I've risen to his challenge, Tom is showing me his places – drains, ditches, pools, swamps – with a real excitement because they are where the recordings of the amazing sounds I've heard come from; they are the source material. With the authority reserved for those whose marrow has frozen for their art, Tom tells me about winter: cracking ice, curlews and the frost-piercing calls of a vixen – ghost of the hanged boatman's lost love. I imagine.

Sunset pours an amber glow like whiskey across the reeds; I look down the purple shadows under the boardwalk and Tom points out a cappuccino cup floating on the quiet slosh of water. Is this a sign of metropolitan confidence or a squalid reminder that Nature is a commodity to be used up and dumped? Unless . . . I get it now. Gerard Manley Hopkins famously stated,

> Of wet and of wildness? Let them be left,
> O let them be left, wildness and wet;
> Long live the weeds and the wilderness yet.

Tom Lawrence says the same thing but he allows the voices of wet and wildness to actually speak for themselves.

As daylight drains into the fen, what's left in the darkness is sound. I understand Tom's recordings of this place are not just an archive; not just one man's obsession with collecting something the rest of us have never experienced; they're a creative response to the presence of this magical place in a hostile world; a cultural standing-up for wild Nature. We're talked out and just lean in silence on the handrail of the boardwalk like a couple of old boatmen, looking over the darkening water, listening to the night in Pollardstown Fen.

The next day I think I'll drive around alone, get a feel for the wider landscape. Instead, the fates conspire to lead me back to the Hanged Man's pub. I walk to the Point of Gibraltar and take the right fork along the East Drain. I watch large heath butterflies – which I've never seen in Britain – and marsh orchids on the bank, then suddenly freeze. Sedge warblers are going mad, cranking up their scratchy calls and fluttering in alarm around a parting of the reeds. There, a fox comes to the water's edge: sharp-faced and fiery, as if to cross and rid herself of this mob of sedgies. She thinks better of it and melts back into the fen and legend. I scramble through the undertangle of fallen willow and sit by the water. Rain begins to fall. I look down and pick up an old broken pencil-sharpener: a useless but strangely enigmatic gift. I listen to the song of rain.

Tom's death came as a shock. He had been back recording at Aylmer's Folly, the famine tower on the Hill of Allen and I suspect, absorbed by its secret sounds, risked the narrow ledge on the battlements at the top. He fell. This was not just a terrible loss for Tom's poor family but of a man whose work was revealing a world the rest of us had never experienced, a world of strange beauty and frightening intensity which, in a way, claimed him. We completed the radio programme *The Water Boatman's Song* for BBC Radio 4, my script speaking for Tom, Pollardstown Fen and his strange and wonderful recordings from another dimension. It is hard for me to think this, never mind write it but I remember Tom's question which referred to his namesake in my play *The Ditch* and although it's conceited romantic nonsense, I feel involved in something darkly overwhelming.

6.
HOLE

An empty space in a solid body; an aperture in or through something; a burrow, cavity or receptacle; an awkward situation; a position from which something is absent.

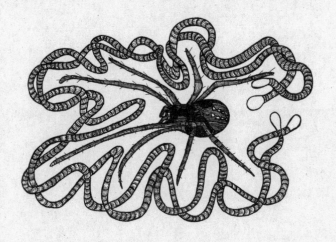

SKRJABINGYLUS

Bang! An explosion in a nearby quarry sounds like a door slamming. The birds are silent for a second or two, then the clatter, caw and cluck of a train of jackdaws echoes off cliff walls. I'm sitting on wooden steps up to Robin Hood's Cave. From here I overlook a long pool in the gorge of Creswell Crags, a ravine riddled with caves on the Nottinghamshire–Derbyshire border. This limestone knoll in the fields and woods of lowland England, sliced by glacial meltwater, looks more like a street of terraced houses than some wild refuge in a mountain fastness and yet it once represented the very edge of human culture. In the pool are mallards and domestic ducks, dowdy and subdued in the eclipse plumage of their summer moult and, in contrast, damselflies stitch electric blue across the pond scum of floating feathers. I'm thinking about the jackdaws and their tenure in this place, how the sound of their society is older than ours.

When Victorian archaeologists dynamited the caves at Creswell Crags to expose layers of habitation under the floors, the jackdaws will have been shocked into silence before exploding into hysteria themselves. I don't know when they first arrived but I imagine jackdaws living in nooks and crannies in the cliffs here when a medieval outlaw society holed up in the caves and when tribal renegades hid from Roman power. In the deeper layers, they were clamouring around Magdalenian hunting groups which followed the herds here across the land bridge from the continent during the Age of Reindeer 14,000 years ago and may have known Creswell Crags as a natural trap used by hunters for centuries. Deeper still, jackdaws swirled around the Gravettian women. These people, named after a French cave, were early Stone Age hunters who left behind the so-called Venus figurines which inspired poetic myths of the Earth Mother and Moon Goddess – the spirit of Nature from which life springs. As a way of recovering that idea, Robert Graves, in *The White Goddess*, cites what he calls *analeptic thought* as a means of throwing his mind back to that time. Using cues from archaeology, literature and the flashback of cultural imagination, Graves creates a speculative mythology of goddess worship which could travel back 32,000 years ago to these caves. The darkness in the cave mouth behind me invites such intuitions, and even though I can't think as a Gravettian or Magdalenian, I wonder if the links between our time and the deep past are through the animals that still share the same place. Are jackdaws a kind of *analeptic thought*? Perhaps they do think the same way now as they thought then. Can they flashback even to the deepest of layers from 50,000 years past, when they knew the people who were not people: the Neanderthals? What could the birds tell us about them: that they were superhuman, heroes, gods, demons? The jackdaws share holes and chimney cracks in the limestone cliffs of Creswell Crags; they dress in its darknesses and sing its songs.

Within the rattling din of calls and wing-beats are the syllables of a language I can only guess at as I listen to the hair-trigger excitement of the train of jackdaws. The animal behaviourist Konrad Lorenz (1970) identified key elements of jackdaw: a song of colloquial calls associated with specific postures together with sounds they imitate from the world around them; the *kia* sound used when sessile or perching; the *kioo* sound when flying and long sentences of repeated syllables when gliding; the *jup* sound for defence against intruders or domineering individuals. Listening carefully, there are many more jackdaw sounds that don't lend themselves to mnemonics because of the clipped, wheezing crackle of their voices. Individual calls are loud enough to penetrate the chorus-squall when they electrify the air with choirs of mob-minded excitement. To me they sound as if individual calls contribute to a common language which is given meaning communally. Together, their collective voice amounts to one bird, with a sound less like words, more like stones falling from cliffs, ice-edged as the iris rings in their eyes. What confronts the ear as an intimidating racket outside the train may sound like a joyous exaltation to the birds inside. They can, however, talk like us. When I lived in Coventry I used to visit a jackdaw in an aviary in the park. Bored, lonely and exiled from its tribe, the jackdaw began to develop relationships with people. It would recognise me, as I'm sure it did others, sidle along its perch to the wire mesh, cock its head conspiratorially and say *Hello?*

As the train of jackdaws rattles off towards feeding fields, their calls hiccupping at the next quarry blast, a warm June quiet fills the gorge. My attention bounces down the wooden steps. The grass is moving; something is moving through the grass. Suddenly a head pops up: ginger, white, jet eyes, a nose, rounded ears, a face fizzing with devilment – a stoat.

For a second, the cute but expressionless gaze surveys the world. I am sitting very still, about 10 yards away uphill and there is no wind. It does not detect me, or if it does it is satisfied there is no threat. The stoat immediately resumes its forensic examination of the ground, focused and hungry, oblivious to anything but the scent trail it has picked up through the grass. This stoat – from 'stout', an old northern European word for 'bold' – is male, a Jack, 10 inches long and weighing about 9 ounces with the sinuous body shape and fluid movement common to many of the Mustelids such as weasels, polecats, pine martens and otters. He also shares a reputation with them as a ferocious killer, the character Kenneth Grahame adapted comically for *The Wind in the Willows* where, with weasels and ferrets, stoats are cast as wrong-uns. Because they will kill and stash the bodies of as many grouse or pheasant chicks as they can catch, they are assiduously trapped as 'vermin' by gamekeepers and used to be hung on fence-wire 'larders'. In New Zealand, where stoats were introduced in the 1880s, despite warnings by British and New Zealand biologists, to control rabbits (introduced in the 1870s), they took to the native forests where they stand accused of threatening populations and species of indigenous birds.

A consummate predator, more than capable of killing a rabbit three times his own weight, he has an eel-like body with short legs and compact head: the perfect physique for a hunter of burrows, tunnels and narrow runs through thicket and hedge. Although largely nocturnal and adept at concealment, stoats are occasionally seen by day, and this one is noticeable. In winter he may be 'in ermine'. During autumn, triggered by the change in day-length, stoats moult their rough, sandy to chestnut-brown summer coat and grow a dense, silky, white one for winter. A white coat makes for perfect camouflage in snow and the stoat evolved as an Ice Age hunter whose range follows the Arctic around the northern hemisphere. But opportunity has allowed it a more temperate distribution and where there's no snow, ermine sticks out like a snowball in a coal shed. Southern stoats may retain brown patches or just turn slightly paler. Apparently, changing to ermine is inherited: a white stoat taken south will not go brown; a brown stoat taken to the Arctic will not turn white. What's unique and common to all stoats is the black tip to its tail, which apart from the difference in size is the diagnostic characteristic which makes a weasel *weasley* recognisable and a stoat *stoatally* different.

Displayed on the ceremonial cloaks of royalty, peers of the House of Lords, academic hoods of Oxford and Cambridge, prelates of the Catholic Church and Lord Mayors, ermine fur is still symbolic of power and privilege. This ermine-wearing elite was satirised by Robert Browning in 'The Pied Piper of Hamelin': 'You hope, because you're old and obese/ To find in the furry civic robe ease?' Nothing about the lives of the previous owners of those ermine coats was easy. Yet, however hard conditions are, stoats have a sex life which gives them a unique, if deviant, edge. A female or Jill stoat may mate with several Jacks in May and June but she delays implantation and her fertile cells go into suspended animation for nine months. Gestation begins the following March and litters of up to thirteen kits are born after about twenty-five days in April or May.

Somewhere in Creswell Crags last spring, a Jill stoat will have given birth to a litter in a small cave or old rabbit hole lined with the fur of her kills. The kits may have had different fathers but none of them will play any part in their upbringing. Even before the kits were weaned, a Jack will mate with her and all her female kits which are sexually mature even at two weeks old but they will not give birth until the following year. Perhaps that's what this one is up to. The Jack's territory encompasses those of several Jills and he scent-marks from glands to announce his presence to would-be rivals. Hunting is an opportunistic business of skill, stealth, luck and an obsessive attention to detail. Although stoats will kill and eat mice, voles, rats, squirrels and birds, here they mainly hunt rabbits. Their technique is legendary. On encountering a rabbit, the stoat rises onto its back legs and fixes it with its gaze, swaying and twisting, leaping and flipping in a 'dance', mesmerising the rabbit. Then it pounces, gripping the rabbit's back with its forepaws and biting into the nape of its neck while scratching with its hind claws. The stoat's teeth are too small to reach the rabbit's spinal column or arteries and the rabbit dies of shock, the stoat lapping its blood before dragging its comparatively huge body into hiding.

Another theory for the stoat's hypnotic dance claims the behaviour is caused by the presence of a nematode, a roundworm called *Skrjabingylus nasicola*. A red worm, *Skrjabingylus* inhabits the stoat's nasal and frontal sinuses. The worm begins and ends in the stoat's nose but in between it undertakes a migration of changing forms. From eggs laid in the sinuses, the first-stage worm larva leaves the stoat in its faeces. These are eaten by, or worm their way into, the

soft foot of the grey field slug *Agriolimax reticulate*. Inside
the slug, the worm larva has to shed the cuticle sheath that
protects it from the slug's digestive juices to allow its cells
to grow. The larvae may do this twice and although there
are many nematode parasites of molluscs, *Skrjabingylus* is
just visiting; the slug is only its intermediate host. To reach
its destination and complete its metamorphosis, the grey
field slug carrying the nematode larva must be eaten by a
shrew, frog or lizard. Once this is achieved, the intermediate
Skrjabingylus inhabits the new paratenic, or travelling host,
inside which it waits for its definitive host. Stoats prefer
rabbits, birds and voles but when they are not available,
shrews, frogs or lizards will be taken and so *Skrjabingylus* can
be ingested. The nematodes migrate along the stoat's spinal
cord to the moist, dark cavities of its sinuses where they
become mature. Most of the infestation will be of large red
females and some smaller males. They will grow and breed,
distorting sinus cavities, creating pressure on the brain and
perhaps introducing special bacteria they have acquired
through their life cycle. The presence of *Skrjabingylus* in
adult stoats is so common perhaps it's a normal condition.
The worms do not kill their host, although some research
from Russia – where stoats are an important fur animal
– suggest high levels of infestation can cause population
decreases. Instead, the stoats learn to live with their parasites;
they remain active and functional, tolerating the damage
wrought by the nematode as they worm into their heads.

Inside the stoat's nose, at the very tip of its existence and the
point where it experiences the world of tunnels and burrows,
is a dark cave writhing with creatures pressing against the
predator's brain. *Skrjabingylus* is no mere stowaway hiding

in the cockpit, it is a controlling, demonic influence. Perhaps to the stoat it feels like a snake pit behind the eyes or like voices schizophrenics hear. Do the worms make the stoat mad? Do they inspire it to do things it would not otherwise do? In this grotesque intimacy, *Skrjabingylus* is that part of the stoat which must transmute through other creatures like a migrating soul to become essential to its being. When transported by ship to New Zealand, the flea parasites of rabbits and hedgehogs did not survive the journey but the nematode stowaways in stoats did and are now integral to the wild population there. And yet, according to scientists studying *Skrjabingylus* in New Zealand, there is no proven link between the nematode and the stoat's behaviour.

Here in Britain, folklore and natural history are full of stories about the legendary dance which whips the stoat into a frenzy of leaping, spinning, twisting contortions while the rabbit freezes in terror. This has been reported even when there is no prey animal around. Young stoats do this playfully, perhaps they learn it from adults under the influence of *Skrjabingylus* or perhaps it's just natural behaviour which becomes pathological later in life as a killing ritual. Imagine hunters watching hunters. The power of the stoat's display against a far larger prey is impressive and I wonder if shamans of early hunting societies were also mesmerised by the stoat's dance. Imitating it would require the kind of gymnastic skill that hunters who have to chase down their quarry revere. But the hypnotic, transformative power of the physical display, where the stoat becomes a kind of supernatural creature, lends itself to ceremonial ritual in which the performer transcends his or her self to enter another state. A modern shaman may call this entering the world of spirits. Anthropologists describe a state of being on the threshold of identity, time and mind achieved through ritual as *liminal*. The dance creates a chaotic place: fluid and malleable. This seems a valid way to describe the stoat's behaviour and supports its mystique. Stoat myths include stories about bloodthirsty slaughter; performing rituals for their own dead; gangs of stoats attacking lonely travellers; animals inhabited by the souls of unbaptised infants. Indeed, stoats are possessed. Over centuries, stoat behaviour has excited imaginations and entered cultures as far apart as Native American, Siberian, Irish, Kani of the Urals and Zoroastrian. How much of these myths have something to do with infestations of *Skrjabingylus* and how much of our own culture can be attributed to creatures that inhabit and possess us in secret ways?

The Jack stoat stops rifling through the undergrowth and raises his head again. He seems uneasy. Quick and fierce as he is, sick or inattentive stoats are preyed upon by foxes and buzzards and they've been persecuted by people for centuries. He recognises the smell of an old enemy and behind his nose *Skrjabingylus* tightens its wormy knot. He passes under the wooden steps below me and bolts towards a hole in the crags.

CAVE SPIDER

The metal grille that protects the entrance to Robin Hood Cave makes it look like a prison, but it's open. A few paces into the mouth I look up to the roof and see animals that appear to be made out of beer bottles. Three European cave spiders, their bodies shiny as dark brown glass, with long hypodermic jaws and dark banded legs, each the size of a circle made by thumb and forefinger, remain still, upside down. Some think these creatures of darkness are evolving to move towards the light where there is more insect prey but it seems likely they are females about to spin incubator cocoons from which their young will venture to new darknesses.

Cave spiders are found in subterranean cavities through-out the Palaearctic region. They are widespread in western and central Europe, particularly in the caves of limestone karst landscapes in the Frankish and Swabian Alps of Germany. Although found in Britain, their distribution is patchy and absent from many parts of the country. These spiders require a constant humidity and a temperature above 7 degrees centigrade. Light averse, they have adapted to other dark places: mineshafts, cellars, hollow trees, railway tunnels. Although they spin webs, these are loose, open-centred drapes which are not used for catching prey. Instead, they hunt woodlice, centipedes, beetles and overwintering butterflies and moths, hanging the bodies of their victims on threads to dangle like trophies.

I watch the spiders but they don't betray their presence with any movement; it's as if they're drawn on the cave roof and it's only staring at them that reveals their form. My guess is the spiders see nothing but feel everything, including my presence in the cave. Their bodies are bulbous, fecund, like the Venus figures of Gravettian women, and they will stay up there until they die. In summer, the female builds a teardrop cocoon, 2 to 3 centimetres in diameter suspended from the roof, which is full of her 300 eggs. She will die guarding it. In August the sac disintegrates and tiny black spiders emerge; they will stay there until the following spring when some will travel to the entrance and away to find other caves and the rest remain in the cave of their birth. They live for two or three years.

These spiders probably came to Creswell Crags with people and have been here for as long as the caves have been occupied. A recent story from the North York Moors illustrates how this process continues today. Archaeologists from Bradford University were surveying Chapel Fell Cave and taking their equipment back to store in an old empty house at Malham Tarn overnight. Ten years later, when the old house was being renovated, a colony of cave spiders was discovered. In a very human way of caring, the colonial ambitions of the spiders were reversed and they were carefully collected and returned to the caves they came from. The stowaway spiders in the chattels of nomadic people travelling from Europe could easily colonise the caves used as shelters or seasonal settlements towards the end of the Ice Age when Creswell Crags was one of the most northerly inhabited places in the world. Were these fellow travellers the origin of arachnophobia?

I have to admit: there's something about spiders which creeps me out – but I'm not sure what it is. There is an electrical charge in spiders capable of causing a shock or at least a hair-raising frisson. I've been very close to black widow spiders and other potentially deadly species in North and South America; they are beautiful and I feel privileged to have seen them. I've been bitten a couple of times by the larger British spiders which have caused no more damage than a temporary sore itch; that sensation is really a privilege, too. However, I do feel an involuntary shudder when a big house spider suddenly runs up my sleeve. Perhaps the most electrifying spider encounter of recent years was watching raft spiders at Wem Moss, in north Shropshire. The largest of all European spiders, raft spiders don't have a raft but walk on water, hunting in small pools on sphagnum bogs. With a body an inch long, their outstretched legs would cover a teacup; they are big enough to kill small fish and tadpoles and they practise sexual cannibalism – females eat males after sex. What I find unnerving is the way they instantly disappear under the surface of the water; they can stay submerged for an hour. Then, creeping slowly and inexorably like Nosferatu, they emerge, long legs heaving their body out onto the meniscus. They move with such sinister grace between the worlds of air and water but inhabit the improbably delicate margin between them. I see the cave spiders in the rock roof above me, poised before the moment they lay eggs, wrap them in a gossamer sarcophagus and stand guard until their own deaths. It's not them that unnerve me, it's the cave spiders that I can't see: the ones that stalk the thin veneer of darkness and can vanish into what lies beneath it.

Spiders in western European culture are fear icons and they inhabit a web of anxieties that are not articulated but concealed. The received wisdom from evolutionary psychology about the origins of arachnophobia is that, together with a fear of snakes, it is a survival response to avoid venomous creatures. This response goes back to early placental mammals, and the primate response of standing and pointing to warn the group is something we have inherited. Although there are many venomous spiders, there are none in western, northern and central Europe that cause serious harm to humans. In many parts of the world where dangerous or deadly spiders do exist, there is far less specific fear of them and spiders are eaten as a delicacy. In the history of the early cave dwellers at Creswell Crags, the other occupants such as cave lion, sabre-toothed cat and cave bear presented a truly terrifying prospect. These great predators are long extinct but the cave spiders remain. Although there is an undiminished appetite to see predators such as big cats, wolves and bears in zoos, on film and in wilderness reserves, arachnophilia is still marginal. Perhaps it's because, like lions and tigers and bears, we too are mammals and although they've hunted us and we've hunted them, we share a warm-blooded history. We admire their ferocity, prowess and courage but we have also managed or destroyed the populations of so-called charismatic megafauna and their habitats to such an extent that the majority of people are not threatened by them; whereas they recognise the threat in us. After all, there are more tigers in zoos in Texas than roam free in the wild. This is not the same for spiders.

Many people without a phobia of spiders say they are repulsed by the way they look and move. The sudden articulation of eight hydraulically extended legs can be surprisingly rapid and their morphology appears alien; more so than beetles or millipedes. Spiders have an unnerving awareness: three pairs of eyes, sensory palps around their mouths, hairs with a sense of touch and proprioception – like hearing and a sense of self, body position, movement and acceleration. Spiders have macabre dietary requirements: they paralyse their prey by injecting venom, bind them up, douse them in digestive juices and suck the broth of nutrients. Spiders spin webs: size for size, gossamer is stronger than high-tensile steel and can be used for making traps, climbing, creating chambers, wrapping prey, egg sacs, holding sperm and flying and appears like magic out of the animal's backside. Spiders have complex sex rituals to prevent, often unsuccessfully, the murder of the male. They are the most other of others and, uninvited, they share our most intimate spaces. What happened in these caves many thousands of years ago happened with cave spiders; they came with people we think of as ancestors and they survive in this ancient darkness, living with secrets scratched into the rock.

We fear the spider and ignore the web. The focus on one fear is a distraction from a much greater and interconnected source of anxiety: arachnophobia diverts attention from a more pernicious and fundamental ecophobia – a fear of wild Nature. Specifically, this is the fear that wild Nature will answer our presence on Earth, our existence and intervention in natural processes, with violence: Nature bites back. This is not just what we *feel* about Nature, this is our experience of how Nature *is*. In response to this fear humans have developed strategies which aim to control Nature, to insulate and protect ourselves from it. As our ability to manage the physical environment increases, so our protective strategies become more aggressive; we retaliate against Nature. There is a sense now that our control of Nature is irrationally oppressive and we have gone too far: too far for Nature and too far for ourselves. And yet we are finding it impossible to pull back, our society shaped by ecophobia continues to be driven by it. In our cultural environment we have developed mythologies that also insulate and protect us by representing Nature as something it is not. Both these strategies – land management and mythology – have their origins in the early inhabitants of these caves. Since then, our strategies of retaliation and representation combine in projects that conceal ecophobia: agriculture, science, society, art, philosophy, religion. The spider spins a thread through Western culture which leads back to the cave.

In the Dark Ages following the decline of the Roman Empire, spiders were thought of as contaminants of food and water and that sense of disgust spills into the modern anxiety disorder of arachnophobia, which (according to Davey 1992) affects as many as 55 per cent of women and 18 per cent of men. Why a fear of spiders should be so prevalent among women suggests a cultural not a biological condition. Could it be that in the shift to a male-dominated society, powerful women as symbolic of wild Nature were feared and oppressed? Arachnophobia is an anxiety disorder encouraged in women and personifying the fear of poison, the entrapping web and sexual cannibalism – a fear of Nature's feminine principle created by an ecophobia which is a fundamental thread of human history. The reason behind it may be irrelevant but fears persist through history.

I watch a cave spider overhead on the cave roof. She is waiting. She is not the Arachne of Ovid's *Metamorphoses*, cursed and humiliated by a jealous Athena; not the pathetic half-spider penitent tortured in Dante's *Purgatorio* for the sin of pride. She is a force of Nature from before she was re-presented under the control of men. She is an aware and living darkness in a web of darkness. At the very least, she makes me jump.

CAVE HORSE

Robin Hood Cave got its name as a refuge for the outlaw of Sherwood Forest – not far away and once linked to Creswell Crags – when he was on the run from the Sheriff of Nottingham. Bars now keep the outlaws out. Stories about turning to the cave for sanctuary are fittingly symbolic for this place. In Abrahamic religions the cave was a sanctuary. In Judaism, David, and in Islam, Mohammed both hid from their enemies in caves. In each of these stories, the cave entrance was sealed by a spider's web which when discovered unbroken was assumed not to harbour the fugitive. In a sort of parallel folk-religion, Robin Hood's messianic role as fugitive medieval bandit, freedom-fighter, defender of the true king and champion of Merrie England's poor gets mixed up with the myth of the Green Man. This pagan symbol of fertility and rebirth is often depicted as a head made of foliage from plants growing out of his mouth, ears and nose – like the stoat's *Skrjabingylus*. He has a varied history of tolerance and prohibition in the Christian Church and is now a common image personifying and, I suppose, de-feminising Nature. There seems an inherent conflict in the Green Man, between his origins in early agrarian societies as the masculine spirit of seasonal regeneration and the growth of crops and his symbolic representation of the wild as a feminine force beyond human governance. At one time – perhaps the moment historians call the Neolithic revolution – the hunter-gatherer and agrarian-pastoral interpretations of Nature separated, and societies shifted from matriarchy to patriarchy. Now, in the environmental crisis created by industrial agriculture, they are worlds apart.

In the many pub signs dedicated to the Green Man, he often appears in the guise of Robin Hood, dressed in Lincoln green, free in the Greenwood – a paternal, protective figure. I used to drink in just such a Green Man: an old, unfashionable pub with few concessions to modern tastes since the days my grandfather delivered beer there. The place on Mill Bank was a dark and dusty sanctuary with the feel of outlaw country; a den for misfits who appeared to belong nowhere else. Although there was nothing extraordinary about it as a pub, perhaps the name Green Man, or *Mon* in local dialect, or the way the building felt so deeply rooted into an ancient place below the roadside, but there was always a feeling like a kind of observance to drink there. It was knocked down, of course; replaced with a little clutch of cheap houses called Green Man Close. Since then, I admit to being a bit sceptical about Green Man this and that. However, behind the commercialisation of heroic myth, Robin Hood and the Green Man do still coexist in a space between Nature deity and fugitive outlaw, although I suspect that to converge so successfully, one of them has had a sex-change.

When Robin and his Merry Men holed up in Creswell Crags, on the run from the law and the corruption of the state in the form of the Sheriff of Nottingham, he entered that darkness in which the stoat dance and other more unimaginable rituals linked ancient people to a world beyond the cave spiders. Robin needed the cave to swallow him as part of his metamorphosis; inside it he was transformed from man to myth, local terrorist deified into Pan-like Nature spirit. Somewhere in there, the female principle as she appeared in the Venus figurines of the Gravettian women 30,000 years ago became the male idea which eventually morphed into the Green Man. And yet I hear a woman's voice here, in some powerfully distant way, as I did in that sad ruined croft on a Scottish island, as in a dream. Caves are places of dreams and transformations and the results of such dreams can still be seen on their walls.

I had been here before to see the earliest example of cave art in Britain first discovered in 2003. I was shown images of animals created 13,000 years ago by nomadic hunter-gatherers on the wall of a cave called Church Hole. I met Paul Petit, an archaeologist who discovered the cave art and was working on fragments of evidence which revealed something about the lives of Ice Age people 13,000 years ago and the Neanderthals who also occupied Church Hole between 60,000 and 40,000 years ago. On the face of it, that's a simple, if amazing story, however extraordinary the cave art is. But something about that cave wormed into my consciousness and began to create a dark space in there. Like a memory that really belonged to someone else, I became more aware that *I knew* the animal image I had seen in Church Hole had a profound significance but was not sure what. Through what Robert Graves called *analeptic thought* about this 'art' I felt it was not just an image of a particular creature; it was more like a cipher: secret marks older than writing, which ancestors used to invoke this place of dreams, the script for a supernatural performance in which people and animals became each other. Did it still work?

Outside, troops of midges danced in sunlight slanting through trees, warming the creamy stone on one side of the Crags. On the shady side of this street, we climbed mossy steps to a metal grille, unlocked it and swung open the gate. Shuffling into sudden gloom, torches threw pale moths of light against stone. More steps up to a metal gantry high against the cave roof represented the original floor level. I couldn't see anything but felt the bare stone drawing me closer. Many things may have changed in 13,000 years but not the darkness of the cave. A beer mat-sized blob of torchlight stuck to the wall and I was being shown some scratchy thing which looked as if kids might have put it there a few years ago. What was it? As I began to make out the shape of it, my imagination was following lines on the rock as if they were the map of a journey scratched into the wall with a flint.

This map began its own narration: sometimes the journey takes a year, sometimes two if the rivers are in spate. It starts here in what might now be called Belgium. They follow the reindeer and other herds across this chalk ridge which is under the sea now and they make a long line, like a tail, then curve along the back, cross-country to where the woods thin out towards the mountains. Then up the A60 between Mansfield and Worksop before turning left on the B6042 called Crags Road. But this is 13,000 years ago, you understand? They come here and make this zigzag like ears and then an oblong under it like a muzzle because this is the head, the place they come to for dreams. The head has no eyes because it doesn't need them in the dark. Then they go back down the neck of this land and the legs travel south to the hoof then back up north, then along the belly sagging with sweet grass and maybe a foal inside there. Now more legs south and north up the great round arse of East Anglia which brings them back to the tail, back along the ridge to the other side where they stop until the weather lets the herds back and they follow them here again. Look at the map now. Let the flame flicker on it a bit. It's the shape of a horse, they belong to this horse and now they've drawn it we can dream it. Listen . . .

We follow the hooves and the singing deeper into the cave until the flame gutters and the darkness holds us tight. Blood, bone, things grown from the ground, only breath and bird wings touch us. We come to the dreaming, following horses like wolves do. We are dreaming this together.

George Stubbs had a dream of horses. When he lived over the way in Lincolnshire studying horse anatomy for his paintings in the 1750s and 1760s, he came to Creswell Crags for inspiration. Stubbs would strip away the layers of horse flesh until he came to the bones and from the bones he would reconstruct his dream of the horse and create a fantasy world for it at Creswell Crags. Rumour has it Stubbs studied bones excavated from caves here for his anatomical studies. But these were not the bones of posh horses, these were bones of Ice Age horses thousands of years old: tough, stocky, bloody-minded nags with wild eyes, slaughtered on the plains of England and dragged back into a dark lair in the rocks. Imagine then, the dream horses George Stubbs painted: *Horse Frightened by a Lion* and *Horse Devoured by a Lion*. These are savage visions which came from dreams here like memories of the Pleistocene lions and *Smilodon*, the sabre-toothed cat, leaping demons from the Ice Age onto the backs of their noble victims, claiming their flesh. Did George Stubbs paint visions which tried to reclaim a wild world from one that had turned against Nature?

American author, poet-philosopher and naturalist Henry David Thoreau had a dream that wild Nature would save the world. One day he sat on Lee's Cliff in Massachusetts and watched another man working with a horse. Thoreau thought it was not being treated as an animal but a machine for pulling carts of dirt. Both the man and the horse had forgotten that horses were ever free. Even wild horses running across the great plains of America were descended from tame ones. The man was just getting work out of the horse as if it were an engine. This made Thoreau sad and he wondered what it would be like if all animals became machines and every squirrel was made to turn a coffee mill and every gazelle pulled a milk cart. But what if that horse dreamed it was free, and because it had stepped out of this darkness a long time ago, it could step back into it again?

We follow the hooves and the singing deeper into the cave until the flame gutters and the darkness holds us tight. Blood, bone, things grown from the ground, only breath and bird wings touch us. We come to the dreaming, following horses like wolves do. We are dreaming this together.

There was another man called George from down the road who had a dream but not quite a dream about darkness. George, who was also called Lord Byron and had a cinema and a pub in Worksop named after him, wrote a poem about the sun going out and people turning on each other until there was only darkness left.

The winds were wither'd in the stagnant air,
And the clouds perish'd; Darkness had no need
Of aid from them – She was the Universe.

He wrote the poem in 1816, in the summer of darkness, a year after the volcano Mount Tambora erupted in South-East Asia, sending a dust cloud that blocked out the sun, plunging Europe into a little ice age. To many people this was a signal of the apocalypse, a sign there was no compassionate god because the bones of ancient animals found in caves were evidence that if Nature could inflict such terrible ordeals and extinctions, it could do so again. They were right. The mammoth, the sabre-toothed cat and the great elk melted away with the Ice Age but we followed the horse from the cave and enslaved it. Now we stand on the edge of an even greater age of extinction.

Ted Hughes the poet had a dream of horses, too. In his dream we are grooms caring for our stabled horses. But wild horses return one night and the sound of their thundering hooves lulls us into a dream and drives our horses mad. We will be punished for this, for not taking proper care of them and time will be marked by the circling of horses' hooves. I think about our dealings with animals; about how we should have devoted ourselves to them. Perhaps the wild ones will come back from the darkness in the end. I see George Stubbs's painting *A Grey Hunter with a Groom and a Greyhound at Creswell Crags*, and see the look that passes between them in this place and all the time there was the cave horse in the darkness behind them.

Everything outside the cave changed and is still changing. Inside Church Hole, in the strangely religious dark, the scratched wild horse survived unchanged for 13,000 years. The darkness survived too. The cave man, the cave horse . . . it's a dream we keep. *We follow them as wolves follow; hear the ghosts of great cats roaring across the tundra; feel the thunder of hooves, smell their hides, watch their breath rise like smoke in the morning; sort through their bones to crack for marrow. We conjure the cave horse. Here, from the darkness, I will draw something for you. Then you can follow it – to freedom, slavery or extinction? Here, I'll scratch a map.*

Like the travelling people following the herds and returning to these caves where their dreams are scratched into animals on the wall – the horse, the auroch, the stag and a bird some describe as an ibis but I think is a curlew – I've come back. I was sitting on the steps outside Robin Hood Cave watching the jackdaws when I saw the stoat. I came inside and saw the cave spiders. I went across the gorge to Church Hole to revisit the Ice Age images of the cave horse, stag and bird. I am here to take part in the modern equivalent of cave art – a television documentary for BBC2 called *The Sacred Wonders of Britain* discussing the images at Creswell Crags. There's a producer, a cameraman, a presenter, a couple of experts and me. I'm here to read a piece I've written about another incised image – a great stag – which attempts to cross the 13,000 years between now and when the animals of the cave art were created in a way that combines the sacred and the profane. I am to be filmed reading it in the back of Church Hole but like most location-based television recording sessions I've been on, most of it is about hanging around waiting and as my part happens last I have time to poke around in caves and daydream.

The darkness has a familiar smell and feel. It has texture and sound. It is not like a darkened room contained within walls, it is a sort of dimension without time or physical boundary: a psychic space. Out of earshot or when people are not talking, there are voices in the darkness: some animal, some human, some both. There is a stillness in the cave which is not passive but transformative. In the caves of my memory, I wriggle through a tight hole under a boulder to emerge into a huge, cathedral-sized space; I dig through a wall of chalk to rescue someone buried behind it; I dangle from a rope above a dark abyss. The most frightening and inspiring cave I ever encountered was one made by blasting hot water into the base of the Engebreen glacier in Norway from hydro-electricity tunnels driven into the mountain. I was with biologists investigating life in extreme conditions: microbes living between ice crystals in the glacier as it ground slowly from the Svartisan ice cap down to the fjord. They were there, locked in tiny fissures for centuries, and for a frightening moment so was I.

The ice cave was smaller than a car. To enter meant scrambling under rocks embedded in the glacier which, if dislodged, would block any exit from the cave. Inside, pistol-shot cracks rang out as the pressure from 50 metres of ice above tried to close the hole up. It was also creeping away from the tunnel. Through this fear of being trapped, crushed and swept away inside the glacier, came a sense of the Pleistocene: a frozen but constantly moving world of such immense power that when it retreated further and further north it revealed a land completely transformed. Now the Engebreen glacier itself was shrinking because of climate change, revealing a kilometre of scarred naked rock above the fjord. This was the result of fear: ecophobia, a human war against Nature which arguably began with the advance of people in the wake of the retreating ice; the attrition of the great predators and the increasing passion for claiming, controlling and management of the new land.

So, the darkness does have a familiar smell and feel. It has a presence that is recognisable 13,000 years after the people left their marks in it for us. It holds that journey. Sitting on a rock ledge at the back of Church Hole with a small light, I read this piece about the stag to the camera:

> Only a moment ago you were browsing birch leaves in the forest. It was all summer wind-sigh, birdsong and the twitch of flies. Until we sent the dogs in.
>
> Then you bolted from the shadows, snorting, mad-eyed, raking branches with your stag head, stamping hooves on rocks so hard they broke and time split open.
>
> All us lot chased after you, through the long years. And we chased you down the railway line to Worksop and up the A60 from Mansfield and people came out of their back gardens and cul-de-sacs and car parks and pubs, cinemas, betting shops and out-of-town-retail-outlets.
>
> They all came to gawp at the Great Stag Do. This was your last night of freedom and we were all roaring drunk in your honour, chasing you down high streets, breaking windows, setting fire to wheelie bins. And every time they cornered you you'd come out swinging – bodies flying all over, every A&E department for 20 miles filled with your handiwork. And you'd jump buildings and clear rivers and sparks would fly. They would never see your like again.
>
> It was only a moment ago, when in a single bound you reached the top of the crags and stood there with the sunset in your antlers and bellowed. The last rutting cry of

a horned god, a great belch of defiance and freedom, the sound the end of an era makes. Then you vanished down Church Hole.

Into that dark place, where we come for dreaming, we scratched your likeness on the cave wall – trying to piece together what happened before the hangover. Flint marks remember: your legs like jackhammers breaking stone, splitting time; your flesh we ate, your blood we drank, your hide we wore, your tendons we laced our boots up with. Then the bone trees which grew from your mind – each tine the branch of a family, our family, a way piercing the future. We used your antlers to quarry stone, mine coal, gouge roads and railways, dig foundations of out-of-town-retail-outlets and our own graves.

In the cave you are still, carried by this scratch on a wall; in the darkness here for 13,000 years – only a moment ago.

7.
SWARM

*A large number of insects, birds, people or spores
in a cluster; moving over or filling a large area; gathering
in large numbers to overrun, crowd or infest.*

PISMIRE

I was on my way into town when I first saw them stumbling out of a hedge onto the street. It was a sunny morning, still and close and about to become hot later. There had been days of this: an uncharacteristically hot and clammy July, not like recent British monsoon summers, although there was a shower last week. Nothing unusual on the street: some morning shoppers buying veg from under the Guildhall, cakes from the baker's, queuing outside the butcher's, fetching newspapers; a few visitors taking photographs, walking dogs; swifts ganging over the bell tower, jackdaws in churchyard trees and the yaffle, a green woodpecker, shouting at sheep in fields beyond the priory. The town was behaving normally for a sunny Saturday morning, oblivious to the metropolis about to spill out from under its hedges and pavements. All I needed from the ironmonger's was some 13 amp fuses, perhaps symbolic of an electrifying moment about to spark up. I rushed back to check my own back garden. They were there too, the pismires: *piss* because their colonies drenched in formic acid smell like urine and mire from the Latin name for ant. They were flying ants.

This was the moment, at least a moment, when quite separate ant colonies synchronised their nuptial flight. In this case, the distance between my garden colony and the one I'd seen under the hedge in town was about 100 yards. There would be others scattered around too, perhaps in other towns, other counties, doing the same thing. At the edge of our garden path, under a fringe of red deadnettle, the black ants were pouring out of the nest. At first they were all piling on top of each other as if in panic, a scrabbling, chaotic mass. It appeared haphazard at first but it soon became obvious that it was organised and purposeful. Tiny worker ants were running protectively around the perimeter while many others seemed to be coaxing the alates – the winged offspring – into the light. First came the drones – the tiny winged males – then the gynes or virgin queens emerged, twice the size of the drones. They all appeared to blunder around drunkenly together until they got the idea of climbing up the plant stems. There was no hanky-panky before take-off, perhaps an obvious strategy to prevent interbreeding, but how these things are determined is a mystery known only to the swarm mind.

The theory is that nuptial flights are triggered by weather fronts creating warm still flying conditions a few days after rain has softened the earth for queens to burrow into and start new colonies. This is certainly true this year: it is still, warm and humid. In recent years the idea of the Flying Ant Day – when all the black ants swarm at once – has been extended into several days in July and August perhaps because the kinds of weather fronts the ants need have been disrupted by other fronts bringing rain. In 2012, a survey carried out by the Society of Biology listed 6,000 reports of flying ants over a two-week period in Britain. In the hot but sporadic summer of 2013, there were four separate flying ant days, the first in June and the last in September. This summer, it seems the ants 'know' there is better weather and what's more they've been preparing for it.

Each nuptial flight involves many colonies and many millions of individuals. How they all perceive ideal weather conditions and act upon it together on the same day suggests communication and planning. A black ant colony can contain 15,000 workers, although smaller colonies of 4,000–7,000 are more common. This Shropshire market town has a population of around 3,000 people in an area of a few hectares. If there was only one black ant nest for each of the 1,400 households, it would mean, at a very conservative estimate, a population of 5,600,000 ants occupying the same space as the people. In reality the total back-garden ant population would be many millions more and, until the nuptial flight, coexist almost invisibly with the human inhabitants. Natural phenomena can still arouse fierce passions. Confronted by something they don't understand and which strikes them as weird, disgusting and on their doorstep, a common response is for people to reach for the Ant Doom – *destroy complete ant colonies without trace . . . discreet and easy to use* – or pour a kettle of boiling water over the seething insects. Catering for this impulse to annihilate the other population of our town, the ironmonger sells a large selection of weapons of mass destruction: smoke bombs, electrocution devices, poison pens, sprays, powders, granules, swats.

I find swarms fascinating, a collective consciousness, like watching a mind thinking. My wife Nancy and I were walking on Wenlock Edge, trying to decide whether to buy a house here when we jokingly agreed we would make the decision based on a sign. Within half an hour we were engulfed in the roar of thousands of wings as a swarm of bees passed overhead and gathered in the branches of a beech tree. We walked right through the swarm; it was electrifying and strangely humbling. We bought the house. Of course I've been stung many times by wasps, occasionally by bees and once had a painful run-in with a swarm of white-faced hornets in America. I have watched murmurations of starlings and clouds of bats in awe. I sympathise with poor farmers enduring a locust migration of biblical proportions but see in the plague a savage beauty. Even more terrifying, I have seen colonies of bacteria swarm into infection or disease proportions under a microscope but feel oddly inspired by them. I don't think this is necessarily a perverse reaction yet it does run counter to the revulsion of the swarm shared by many in Western society. However, human social attitudes, particularly to social insects, are ambiguous.

The work ethic and selfless sociability of ants may be admired as qualities of fascinating but mindless automatons, until the robots appear intentional. Hundreds of ants marching across the kitchen floor and getting, literally or metaphorically, in your pants, quickly provokes ecophobia which is fundamental to preserving civilisation. 'Buzz Off! Family forced to eat under a mosquito net after swarms of flies invade Avonmouth' (*Daily Mail*). 'Beemageddon – school closed, shoppers attacked and car covered as swarm of bees cause chaos' (*Mirror*). 'Thousands of Wasps Found in UK Home Devouring Bed' (*abc News*). 'Ginormous Jellyfish Swarm England' (*gogo News*). Swarms represent Nature out of control. There is a tipping point into panic somewhere between many and too many, any large number of ants, bees, jellyfish, toads, bats, sparrows or locusts.

This horror of the swarm might have to do with the sheer numbers of creatures in one place or doing something strange when a lesser number of the same thing would appear beautiful. Take mayflies: they spend a year in the mud of slow-moving rivers and streams, moulting through different stages until the adults all hatch together, then they take to the air to mate, the females lay eggs in the river and they are all dead in forty-eight hours. One spring, Nancy and I went to Ironbridge to see the River Severn when the water level was at an all-time low. As tyres screeched along the Wharfage, we dropped down behind the car park into a silent cloud of mayflies, glimmering with golden light above the water. By the time the sun set behind the cooling towers of the power station, the swarm had vanished, washed downriver. The next morning felt like a change in the seasons and by afternoon a gang of swifts were screaming around the church tower – they had come back from their travels. The swifts brought new weather and a soft, scent-releasing rain. The suddenness in the sky was charged with swashbuckling clouds and a rain of mad birds, gold swarms and iridescent wings. These things were not just loose ephemera but essential elements of a seasonal shift which opened the sky to summer.

In the Midwestern American town of La Crosse on the northern reaches of the Mississippi river in Wisconsin, the seasonal change heralded by mayflies provoked headlines: 'Massive swarm of mayflies terrorise Wisconsin residents' (*Tech Times*). A hatch of mayflies last year was so enormous it was visible on weather radar with echo values similar to that of light or moderate rain over the northern Mississippi area of Wisconsin. This huge cloud of insects initially dispersed up to 2,500 feet into the air. Then they descended. Attracted to the bright lights of La Crosse, other small towns and traffic, the mayflies were forced to adapt their dance of creation to a strange world. They laid eggs in beer glasses; dropping dead they piled up 2 feet thick on roads forming a slick described as *treacherous*.

As well as a fear of the innumerable, there is an anxiety about what the individuals in the swarm are doing. This is encouraged by the comparison between human and insect societies. While some of these comparisons are true for all social animals, there is something about ants that is particularly vulnerable to the legacy of imperialism and the Cold War. Stoked by horror films, science-fiction stories and political morality tales, our society responds to the swarm with a xenophobic fixation on *hordes*. These brainwashed automatons, controlled by some fiendish dictator, ideology or religious belief, are terrifying because they have no individual conscience, no fear of death. This becomes an underlying trope for the 'worker' ants: mindless communists serving a hive intelligence or uncannily organised subjects serving a reclusive queen. Armed with jaws, phenomenal strength and chemical weapons – the piss-smelling formic acid – workers attack or defend, go to war, raid other colonies, hunt and supply the colony with food: nectar, insects, the bodies of their own dead, neighbouring ants and have, like us, a special fondness for sugar. The demarcation of roles and differentiation of larvae into castes of workers, alates and one controlling queen has something to do with the attention workers give to the ant larvae. Winged gynes are groomed; unfertilised eggs, in ant-irony, become drones. Worker ants are nominally female but never sexual. They will only tolerate one paternal queen and any other competing queens in the colony results in conflict and matricide. The queen is single parent to the entire colony. She lies on her side popping out eggs which are taken to nursery chambers where they are cared for by other workers. This sounds like a factory: the perfect metaphor for an industrialised, militarist society. What we feared about hostile foreign hordes turns out to be a fear of ourselves.

On Flying Ant Day, the workers of each contributing colony prepare tunnels from the subterranean chambers where a huge batch of pupating larvae emerge as alates or queens which the worker ants usher to the surface. The moment of confusion when the emerging alates are suddenly exposed to daylight is understandable. These newly adult ants carry different genomes; they have become fundamentally different creatures from their larval selves. After months of blind, soft-bodied helplessness like opaque sausage rolls crowded into dark subterranean chambers and attended by workers feeding them regurgitated juices, the larvae have emerged with great strength, a protective exoskeleton and wings. They are then hustled into a warm, humid, overcast day. They stumble around as if sobering up, getting their bearings, then begin to climb surrounding plant stems. Those in my garden scramble tentatively up red deadnettle stems and grass blades that are not very tall. There doesn't seem much of a pattern to this and the first drones and gynes climb haphazardly away from the nest. The workers seem to leave them alone once they move upwards and, perhaps following chemical trails left by the pathfinders, the other evacuees head for somewhere they can launch into the air. When they do become airborne, everything changes. The wings, particularly those of the drones, are not strong but in the still warm air they do propel the ants upwards. As they climb higher and individuals from different colonies swarm in the same column of air, the gynes release a pheromone that drives the drones crazy. They chase the gynes through the air to mate with them and in that moment deliver enough sperm for the queen to use for the remaining fifteen years of her life, while tearing out their own insides in a fatal ejaculation. Each gyne flies back to earth to find a hole under stones or slabs or dig a tunnel into the soil, make a chamber, bite off her own wings and begin laying eggs, some of which she will have to eat to survive. The others will become the first generation of the new queen's workers.

Can the drones know they are 'sexual missiles' who will explode and die on mating? Do the gynes, who will have to survive on the stumps of their wings and cannibalism in an anchorite cell underground, know they may have to fight their own daughters to the death? Do the dutiful workers hear the screaming gang of swifts overhead, waiting to devour the cloud of flying lovers? How can any of us foresee the wonderful, terrible lives we carry with us?

The flying ants may have swarmed but the colony is linked by mysterious means to surrounding colonies, a population rippling underground across the land and agents of a massive, hidden swarm. The black ants' nest under red deadnettles by the path settles into its regular routine: the queen laying another brood, the workers guarding, nursing, foraging and climbing about in the roses and honeysuckle growing up the fence behind, searching for aphids. Ants milk aphids. Instead of killing and carrying them off, they stroke the aphids gently with their antennae until they exude droplets of honeydew which the ants collect as food for the colony. Honeydew, the stuff which drops from trees to make a sticky mess on pavements and parked cars and often has a sooty mould growing on it, is created by the aphid piercing the phloem tissue which transports the plant's nutrients with its syringe-like mouth and getting a squirt of sap straight into its gut. What it gives off as waste from its back end is highly nutritious and sugar-rich. This is the dew that fell from Yggdrasil, the ash tree at the centre of Norse cosmology which Odin hung himself on and from which bees made a magical honey. Trophobiosis is a symbiotic relationship between organisms based on food. The ants want the honeydew and the aphids need protection. When the ants are around to milk the aphids, they deter ladybirds, wasps and other predators. This is one of the earliest observed examples of symbiosis and appears in ancient Chinese texts. I go to see an example of another black ant trophobiotic relationship which is even more complex and wonderful.

SILVER-STUDDED BLUE

A buzzard cruises high above truck stops at the junction of the A49 and A41 south of Whitchurch in north Shropshire. It veers over the massive grainstore hangars and out across Prees Heath Common. My grandfather, who came from a farm a few miles away, pronounced it *Priz Yeth*, in a dialect that was already fading before the birch trees grew on the remains of the runway. The buzzard follows the line where Second World War Lancaster bombers once lumbered off on deadly missions. From that height, the buzzard can see all that remains of the great heath which once stretched for miles. Prees Heath Common is now hemmed in by thundering trunk roads and a grubby prairie of arable agriculture.

The heather, grasses and other heathland plants moved back onto the deserted airfield after the war. The runways, too difficult to remove, became overgrown but beneath broken concrete, colonies of black ants live to continue their affair with silver-studded blue butterflies, so-called because of light-blue reflective scales on the undersides of their wings. In summer, the butterflies lay their eggs singly like tiny white buttons close to the ground where the temperature is higher and ants can find them on the stems of foodplants such as heather, ling, horseshoe vetch and bird's-foot-trefoil. The eggs will stay there all winter with the larvae developing inside them. When the apple-green caterpillars hatch out they are attended by black ants, which milk them for honeydew and protect them from parasites and predators. The caterpillars pupate in silk-lined chambers underground. Sometimes the ants carry them into their nests and sometimes they form small temporary nests around the pupae for two or three weeks until they emerge. In July, the ants usher the butterflies to the tops of plants where they take off into the heath, but they don't go far. Silver-studded blues remain close to their place of birth, close to the fostering ant nests which raise countless generations of the butterflies, and may only travel in a

20-metre radius during their whole lives. The adults fly in July and August, feeding infrequently on heather bells and other flowers. The butterflies will roost together and can form little clouds of brilliant blue when they disperse in the morning.

I've only ever seen a few individuals at a time and never seen a cloud of silver-studded blues but I imagine a summer morning when my grandfather was a boy, riding across *Priz Yeth* on his horse Tom. This was before the Great War and the Depression, before the airfield was built for the Second World War, a world in which the Common had hardly changed in a thousand years. I imagine the boy Eric looking down on a shimmering blue smoke of butterflies drifting over the heather around Tom's hooves, a faery enchantment.

On a warm but overcast July day, I strain to hear bees and crickets on Prees Heath Common drowned out by traffic on the A49. My generation's return to the heath is like walking through the ruins of an ancient cinema trying to imagine the wonder of films once shown there from fragments of cellulose left in the rubble. Some meadow brown butterflies and burnet moths are in the air but it is not until I come across an island of purple heather that I see any silver-studded blues. A female is dark and silky with a vibrant blue edge and bright copper spots in her hindwings. A male, flying low over heather, has a brilliant blue 30-millimetre wingspan with black margins and white fringes. The creature flashes as the sun appears, a little strobing sapphire light. There do seem to be worryingly few here. Whether the story of the affair between black ants and silver-studded blue butterflies is that of exploitation or devotion, it's a symbiotic relationship which, to be sustained, requires an old ecology: the mesh of stories that can only be told by an entire heath.

It takes a heathen to love a heath. Their wild open spaces are made more mysterious by the wild secret life going on in them and their history is that of hiding places for an ancient but marginalised society of bandits, travellers, fugitives and the dispossessed. Where I lived in Homer, once a common on Wenlock Edge, its earlier inhabitants were described in a nineteenth-century survey as 'idle and extravagant persons'; this is surely a demographic to aspire to. Heaths are the rough and ready antidotes to industrialised countryside. Prees Heath Common is now a reserve of Butterfly Conservation to protect the only population of silver-studded blues left in central England. The butterfly only occurs in a few other locations in North Wales and south-west England and is emblematic of a world that has been disappearing for many years; lost faery enchantments. As conservationists struggle with a changing environment to reclaim more heath, it's not the land alone which matters. For heaths to stand a chance of a future, it's those which dwell on them that count; heaths will not be heaths without the return of the heathens.

On Prees Heath Common, quite different groups of people appear. Dog-walkers drive in, take their lolloping, sniffing, piddling companions out along the footpaths, then drive off. A couple of men who may have been travellers prospecting for a pitch pull up in a flatbed truck. They eye the site carefully then leave quickly. A group of middle-aged people assemble at the gate with butterfly nets and earnest conversation: amateur naturalists.

A year before I met Prees Heath's warden Stephen Lewis. 'Butterfly Conservation bought the Common after a twenty-year campaign to save it from gravel extraction because it's the last site in the Midlands for the silver-studded blue butterfly,' he said. 'Less than 10 per cent of the 60 hectares is relatively undisturbed heath of common heather, bell heather, gorse, broom and fine grasses.' The rest of the Common was being restored by turning the fertiliser-polluted soil over with metre-deep ploughing, removing scrub and seeding heather from other heaths in the region. Lewis said, 'We can replace the old heath with something similar but not identical. Conservation is the prime driver of this project and all our work is linked to the UK BAP (Biodiversity Action Plan) for the silver-studded blue butterfly; it's a flagship species and we will do everything we can for them.'

Prees Heath Common is fairly typical of much of Britain's heathland: a fragment of the 16 per cent of iconic landscape from the nineteenth century that survived into the twenty-first. Heaths were shaped by a way of life which has largely vanished – burning heather and gorse, grazing sheep, cattle and horses, cutting peat turves for fires. When these practices stopped in the twentieth century it dragged some of our most cherished wildlife over the brink of extinction with them. RIP the heath puffball, a unique fungus unseen since 1983. In England there are 133 species with Biodiversity Action Plans of particular importance associated with heathland but only 9 per cent of them actually need heather. Most of them just need openness. Lizards, for instance, need bare ground to warm up or cool down. Heathland species require a particular structural diversity which requires colonising trees to be cut down and runs counter to natural ecological processes. Heaths were often decried as outlaw country, venues for the unnatural, unlawful and uncivilised practices of the villainous. An infamous heath with a controversial past is Greenham Common in Berkshire. It is a stronghold of a very rare, secretive bird with a rough, creaky song called the Dartford warbler. This bird is a true heathen and toughs it out in the harsh conditions of the heath all winter instead of migrating to Africa like other warblers. It was reduced to just a few breeding pairs in Britain and is slowly increasing. It is hard to imagine a spirit more at odds with the American B-52 nuclear bombers which were based at Greenham Common when the Peace Camp existed on its boundary. As at Prees Heath, many heaths became appropriated by agencies of war. The drama of the Greenham Common women's protest against the military was inspiring to me and very much part of the advocacy for a wild Nature which, in restoring the ecology of a heath, also begins to heal wounds in society and right wrongs.

'The Law locks up the Man or Woman who steals the Goose from off the Common but sets the greater Felon loose who steals the Common from the Goose,' says the seventeenth-century rhyme. Commons came to be seen as commonwealth in the freedoms of landless people and wildlife. For most people, the heath commons-as-livelihood connection disappeared long ago and has been replaced by an aesthetic. I love their big skies, the edgy agoraphobia of their wild, weird openness in which the sandy earth holds the heat and the unnerving presence of vipers. Even Prees Heath with its traffic noise and mournful history, still has a corner of its *Priz Yeth* charm in which the silver-studded blues survive. From South African fynbos to Californian chaparral, heathlands are largely open ecosystems of dwarf shrub vegetation on free-draining soils. In the UK particularly, which holds most of Europe's surviving examples, heaths are anthropogenic: short, ericaceous – heather-dominated vegetation that has been maintained by swailing – clearing woodland, burning and grazing – since about 6000 BC. By the eighteenth century, the great expanses of open heaths of the British lowlands were condemned as ugly outlaw country, except by the rural fringe. William Cobbett, political commentator and countryside explorer, detested the 'rascally heaths' near Marlborough. The British Agricultural Revolution sought to cultivate them and by the nineteenth century, heathland champions such as Thomas Hardy were worried about the loss of mystery and freedom on what he called Egdon Heath in his novel *The Return of the Native*, which in reality covered 50,000 hectares between Dorchester and Bournemouth and was suffering from: 'The attempts – successful and otherwise – at cultivation on the lower slopes, which intrude and break up the original heath into small detached heaths . . . which now exclude the cattle of those villagers who formerly enjoyed rights of commonage thereon, and the carts of those who had turbary privileges which kept them in firing all the year round, were not erected.'

Most British heathland is common land, a relic of an ancient communal farming practice dating back at least to medieval times, becoming legally recognised with the Commons Act of 1285. Common land is privately owned but with other people having certain traditional rights to use it in specified ways: such as grazing livestock, gathering firewood or turbary – digging turf or peat for fuel. A continuity of these traditional practices – such as control of the number of grazing animals, the frequency of burning areas to restore heather and grass, refraining from ploughing and fencing – maintained a landscape which then supported the people's rights, and indirectly wildlife, over time. 'Ye commons', wrote the nineteenth-century poet John Clare, are 'left free in the rude rags of nature'. Not any more they're not.

During the twentieth century, the social changes affecting common land practice and the pressure on 'wastes' to be productive led to the massive erosion of wildlife and habitats. Encroachment by agriculture, housing development and conifer plantations wrecked 84 per cent of lowland heath. In 2000, with lottery funding, the Tomorrow's Heathland Heritage project set out to reverse heathland loss and start clawing some back. When the project finished some years later it had restored 42,000 hectares around the UK. The Forestry Commission announced it would be clearing conifers from heathland in England – which holds two-thirds of all UK heaths – at a rate of 1,000 hectares per year with an ambition to restore a potential 30,000 hectares. This will create larger blocks of landscape and help connect up habitats: great news for Dartford warblers, nightjars, wood larks, smooth snakes, sand lizards, silver-studded blue butterflies, ladybird spiders and marsh gentians, trapped in conservation ghettos of fragmented heathland nature reserves. It has encouraged the RSPB to reintroduce the field cricket – a flightless chirruper of sandy heaths, once described as abundant by Gilbert White in 1761 but almost extinct by 1990 – to restored Farnham Heath in Surrey and Pulborough Brooks in West Sussex.

But the world has changed radically in recent years. The main challenges to heathland restoration are nitrogen, from agricultural fertilisers and traffic emissions, like those pouring from the exhausts on the roads strangling Prees Heath, which favours the grasses which out-compete heather; climate change, where plants in warmer summers grow faster creating more biomass and so intensify management requiring more resources to keep the habitats open; and loss to agriculture and development demands for more housing. These processes generated by the urban swarm may become overwhelming for even the most protected heaths but for now it's the pismires, the ants under the derelict runway which are the real conservers of these rare and beautiful butterflies.

SHINING GUEST

Pismires, unsurprisingly given their name, have never been part of the human diet in these islands, unless I count the time I ate some ant eggs and grubs in the spirit of culinary adventure or the rock legend Ozzy Osbourne who allegedly snorted a line of walking ants as if they were a line of cocaine. Otherwise, ants are eaten by specialists such as green woodpeckers and generalists such as badgers. However, some of the most fascinating predators of ants are ants themselves. I do not know if ants feel fear; I imagine their defensive capabilities – such as the formation of military castes, the collective organisation needed for attack and counter-attack and the use of bodily and chemical weapons – have evolved from something like a fear of predators or competition with other colonies. For the black ant, a real danger comes from an enemy it has no evolutionary preparation for. *Lasius niger*, the black ant, should live in fear of its deadly doppelgänger *Lasius umbratus* but it does not. This yellow version of the black ant looks very similar but is almost exclusively subterranean and so seldom seen. Its name *umbratus* means *ghost* and it's a parasite of *Lasius niger*. Black ants cannot detect the presence of *L. umbratus*, they only see themselves. Black ants don't believe in ghosts.

A ghost queen wanders over the ground following scent trails to a colony full of her unsuspecting victims. With great strength she carries the corpse of a black ant worker she has killed in her jaws. She is drenched in the worker's scent which carries all the biometric information about the worker's identity, status and origin, as personalised as a retina scan or fingerprint. Disguised, the ghost queen uses this scent as the key into the colony and the black ant workers are tricked into allowing her through into the inner sanctum. All they detect is another worker. Once inside the ghost queen hunts down and kills the black queen and takes her scent, as potent as the robe, sceptre and crown. Without question, the black ant workers then care for the ghost queen; she lays batch after batch of eggs, thousands of ghosts which will eventually take over the colony. How the ghost ants get away with this, how they infiltrate by disguising themselves with the scents or pheromones of their victims so the black ants adopt them is the stuff of science fiction.

In the various remakes of films based on Jack Finney's 1955 novel *The Body Snatchers*, a small town is infiltrated by seeds from alien pods which take people over, turning them into dehumanised, expressionless automatons that can't reproduce and which will die in five years until all that will remain are the aliens. Loaded with paranoia about communism, McCarthyism, novel diseases, terrorism and nuclear war, *The Body Snatchers* has an alien swarm leading to the end of human existence. In the ant story, in a bizarre parallel, the ghost ants disguise themselves as black ants to eventually wipe them out so that only ghost ants survive. And like the *The Body Snatchers* – in which the modified humans have their own telepathic *grouptalk* which only they understand – the ghost ants must have a means of communication, a *grouptalk* – perhaps chemical or behavioural – which black ants can't comprehend. Does this happen in the world around us? Is there a kind of *Homo umbratus*, a swarm of ghosts hiding in plain sight, versions of ourselves we cannot see because they disguise themselves so well? Ghosts, spectres, spirits, shades: are they just images of ourselves or are they parasitic or symbiotic inhabitants of a parallel world in our midst?

There is a ghost that haunts the most dangerous of swarms in the woods. I stand at the edge of a glade as slats of sunlight lean through the tall masts of a spruce plantation. A couple of silver-washed fritillary butterflies semaphore across sunbeams. I catch a movement in the shadows and stay motionless, watching a roebuck walking cautiously with a hind along the edge. They skirt the glade and take a path to a small clearing between trees. I can hear the sound roebucks make at rutting time, a kind of barking throaty cough, like a bad chest, but it's not coming from the deer I see. He stands for a moment as if watching me but he either can't see or smell me because he rubs his thorny antlers against a sapling, scent-marking. The deer move off and I follow slowly, walking on a narrow path not made by people. I come to the clearing where I last saw the roebuck and stand still to look around. There's a sudden movement on a bare patch of ground and I see a spider hunting. As I watch to see what it's chasing, a small twig begins to move into the open as if by levitation. Looking closely, the twig is being carried by an ant. The twig is five times as long as the ant and it takes five minutes to carry it 30 centimetres. I lift the twig with ant attached carefully and look at the ant through a hand lens. The ant opens its massive scimitar jaws and squirts formic acid so suddenly I almost drop it. This is a wood ant; in close-up, one of the most formidable creatures in the forest. I replace the ant and its stick where I found it so it can continue its journey and I pick up the trail of other wood ants carrying small and dismembered insects heading back to a nest mound 10 metres away under a tree. This one is small for a wood ant nest, about the size of an upturned bucketful of twigs, leaves and pine needles, each of which has been individually collected and positioned by a worker such as the one I interrupted. The nest seethes with ants. They're Britain's largest, over twice the size of black ants, about 10 millimetres long with black heads and abdomen, a red thorax and black legs – impressive, dangerous and with a fearsome reputation.

When deer melt into shadows, butterflies fold up and birds are still, there is a white noise, soft as rain, caused by the movement of millions and millions of wood ants.

Each nest has a colony of between 100,000 and 400,000 individuals. The one I've found is a recent construction, probably a daughter nest formed after their spring nuptial flight. Wood ants have colonies with several nests and up to a hundred queens. Nest splitting happens when workers, queens and brood are transferred from the original nest to a new one and this nest looks like one of those. How did the ants find the new nest site, decide which individuals would be recruited to it and execute the migration? The new nest will have a relationship with the old one and the rest of the colony and the foraging territory will have to change. This shows a colony capable of collecting and distributing large amounts of information as if it were one living thing, not hundreds of thousands of separate mechanical reflex automata. Biologists say the allocation of tasks in a project like this may be down to algorithms – mathematical formulae for solving recurring problems – using variations between individuals and their ability to change behaviour. This idea gets those interested in artificial intelligence very excited. Ants may have no more idea of our intelligence than we have of the 'intelligence' of climate, plate tectonics or evolution. Ants, like us, learn from their environment; they think collectively and individually. This complex decision-making has been compared to that of the brain which does the same thing through the action and interaction of neurons.

Looking at the parallels between primate brains and ant colonies, scientists such as Nigel Franks from Bristol University suggest that separate populations – neurons in the brain, ants in the swarm – gather information to make alternative choices between things. When one population reaches a threshold, a decision is made for the corresponding alternative. This threshold varies because it's a compromise between the speed and the accuracy of the decision-making, which is produced by direct competition between populations of ants in which individuals are gathering information. This evidence-accumulating behaviour in ant populations moving around occurs just like those neurons in the cortex from different parts of the brain. The neurons fire off at rates based on the stimulation of certain brain cells and when the neurons in our brains reach a threshold, our behaviour changes. However, members of the ant population are not just couriers of information. They have been shown capable of flexible behaviours, they learn things, not just in response to the availability of food but also how to use tools and plan. From the information they collect, ants create mind-maps. They hold these cognitive landscape maps individually and share them as a community.

At the centre of their map is home: their mind's nucleus swarms with thousands, fussing around with twigs and leaves, engineering, building, constantly adjusting. Inside, thousands more are teeming in galleries and travelling underground. I cannot tell what they're doing, only that they have a shared intention which is so strong it feels overwhelming and makes no more or less sense to me than human traffic at work and commerce in the streets of densely populated cities. Further thousands of foraging worker ants travel overground. I follow strings of them through the wood, using the narrow trail the roe deer walked, for about 70 metres before the ants peter out. The ones I do not see are up in the trees, milking aphids for honeydew or harvesting them and other insects and spiders and bringing them back to feed the nest colony. This activity alone contributes to the structure of the forest, controlling the influence of leaf-munching insects in the canopy. Each forager can memorise the locations of where and when food is plentiful. Each ant can orientate herself to the direction to and distance from the nest like an iron filing in a magnetic field. Each can take a snapshot of landmarks along the route and memorise a library of these places in a map-like representation of positions relative to the goal – home or food – and the position of the forager. Finding short cuts to work or home and alternative routes back from being disoriented or knocked off course by rain, wind or some idiot picking you up and staring at you with a magnifying glass, is learned like satnav. Ant scouts discover the whereabouts of other nest sites where they can recruit new members to the breakaway colony and persuade them to help with removals. Scouts also know where the dangerous, hostile sites to avoid are.

All the information collected by these activities is stored in pheromone deposits inside and outside the nest. Individual ants can recognise the distinctive odour of the nest, their nestmates and queens. They are super-predators, taking millions of organisms from the wood each day to feed their vast colonies and have a profound ecological effect. They will attack anything which threatens them, having a powerful bite and spraying formic acid. They are also highly aggressive with each other, especially over territory that is based on foraging patterns which are guarded and fought over. The white noise, soft as rain, is the wood ant swarm, walking, working, fighting, killing, thinking.

The presence of a small defenceless creature which inhabits the heart of these ant fortresses, inside the collective mind, is therefore astonishing. The shining guest ant is tiny compared with the wood ant; it's only 3 millimetres long, amber in colour with a dark abdomen, smooth and very reflective, like polished glass. The shining guest ant colonies consist of only about a hundred individuals in a hollow plant stem or bracken frond inside the wood ant nest. They stay inside their own nest until gynes and drones meet on the surface of the wood ant's nest. After mating the queens fly to another nest to begin a colony or stay to start another in the same nest. The males continue to move about on the surface with the wood ants which ignore them. Sometimes a guest may be grabbed but released unharmed, very rarely are they attacked. If a wood ant nest moves, the shining guest ants follow, their workers carrying the larvae and pupae to the new nest. Inextricably linked to the most dangerous of predators, the shining guest ants live in their hosts' nest invisibly like the Borrowers. Perhaps the shining guest has a pheromone which mimics the wood ants and so cloaks it and, like ghost ants in the black ant nest, the odour is an identity theft the host completely believes. Perhaps wood ants see their own reflection in its mirror-like body of the guests and believe they are looking at other wood ants. But how this subterfuge evolved is a mystery. The shining guests are peaceful poltergeists, protected by the wood ants' blind spot. It is hard to see how the host community has anything to gain from their guests.

It is tempting to think that because the shining guest ants have no effect on the wood ants, they are of little importance, an accident of evolution. However, as the philosopher Wittgenstein said, important things become hidden because they are so simple and familiar: 'One is unable to notice something – because it is always before one's eyes.' The shining guests move around like ghosts, unseen. Seeing is believing. We believe the evidence of our own eyes, like the ant colony and the brain neurons we gather information which we act upon believing our thoughts are autonomous. But they are at root a collective thinking, an unconscious. Human existence is so all-encompassing that while watching ourselves and each other we miss the glimmer of other existences. Maybe we underestimate the savage wood ants. Perhaps they have an unconscious awareness of the shining guests. Perhaps they see them as a kind of wildlife and like us they can draw a distinction between the wildlife they exploit and destroy and wildlife they love. Maybe we are the ones who should look closer for the ghosts that dwell among us; the shining, strange and beautiful guests of our own swarm.

8.
ISLE

*Small island or peninsula surrounded by water;
anything compared to an island and surrounded
in some way; a detached or isolated thing.*

STEARNAN

In the house next to BEACHCOMBER FAMILY AMUSEMENTS, PRIZE BINGO & CAFETERIA, the Velux windows in the roof face east. The view from the windows is divided into layers, nearest at the bottom, furthest at the top. The first is the promenade wherein silver-grey cars are parked and police vans patrol. The second is a lawned green wherein forty starlings share the same thought about arriving and departing. The third is a footpath wherein a woman in a red anorak stands under a lamp post with her West Highland terrier wearing a blue coat. The fourth is a beach wherein gull corpses lie on their backs, their heads buried. The fifth is a glittering expanse of wet sand wherein thirty little ringed plover proceed in a southerly direction over a zillion lugworm casts, which stitch the Kingdom of Fife to the Firth of Forth. The sixth is the North Sea wherein a group of eider ducks, enough to stuff a duvet, sleep on the swell as a lone minke whale breaches again and again northward. The seventh is the dark strip of horizon wherein lies the gannet city of Bass Rock like a half-popped cork and, behind the headland, the Isle of May. The eighth is a grey sky wherein the ruin of a hurricane lowers.

We are hiding from Bertha. My family and I have rented a house on the seafront which is just now in the path of a storm raging across the country. Bertha was spawned in the annual tropical cyclone formation in the Atlantic basin and first seen as a tropical wave south of the Cape Verde islands on 26 July. Upgraded to tropical storm then a hurricane – B in the alphabetical sequence – Bertha became a reincarnation of the first hurricane Bertha of 1956. Her moniker may have come from Big Bertha, the huge German guns used in the Great War named allegedly after a Krupp heiress. Appropriately, Bertha blasted the Lesser and Greater Antilles, the Turks and Caicos Islands and the Bahamas before booming up the east coast of the USA and banging off into the Atlantic. Satellite images showed Bertha as a huge, dishevelled whirlpool of wind and water energy. Instead of blowing out, she picked up power over the Atlantic and by the time she hit the British Isles she could smash up trees, flood roads, barrel in waves and hammer on the promenade windows. On the night of high spring tides and a huge full moon, Bertha swirls above as an island of storm; she roars, splutters and then shakes herself out like a wet shag.

The windows open horizontally to the view and I could call out to passers-by on the promenade but I don't know anyone here. I have met some interesting dogs in the last few days, though: four greyhounds, two malamutes, several westies and a young pit bull named Alex. This is a good place for dogs: they chase around on the beach, crash in and out of waves just like holidaymakers, if there were any. The beach is swept clean of their piss-tags by tides. The renewed shore, different twice a day, is a territory that has to be constantly reclaimed by dogs; it's a proprietorial ritual without which ownership of the beach would revert to the malicious oystercatchers. The amusement arcade next door has few punters. The Action Adventure Zone is closed. There's a bouncy castle on the prom for child access weekends. I've been to the Lidl and the chip shop behind the bus station but pass the pubs warily, attracted to the warmth, noise, emotional outbursts and music of the rougher ones but put off, probably wrongly, by the potential hostility. I have the feeling they are ghostly apparitions of proletarian drinking dens from before the reconstruction of the town centre, an archipelago of boozy mischief surrounded by depressed twentieth-century development. A snooty woman in a posh shop in a nearby fishing village tells customers this town is *unexciting*. I don't believe her. Surrounded by pretty, well-to-do and civilised country, this place is a blot. I come from a town like this.

Drawn to the Highlands and Islands, which feel part of the western Britain I identify with, I have never been to eastern Scotland before. Here in the ancient Pictish kingdom, Fib, Fif, or Fife is a peninsula east of the Ochil Hills, south of the Firth of Tay and north of the Firth of Forth. The peninsula points east and my gaze follows it into the North Sea. Although I'm usually landlocked and see sunrise and sunset as an arc between hills, my feelings for that westerly journey are full of memories of holidays on the Welsh coast watching the sun sinking into the Irish Sea. Walking on the beach here, it's strange for me to see the sunrise out of the sea and sunset inland, it's like driving on the right, feels slightly disorientating at first. My British Isles face west. Even though moving westwards is backwards from the direction the world is spinning, it still feels like facing the future. Here in Fife, the British Isles turn to the east, to the past. I want to go to islands out there, to wild Dark Age isles in the North Sea, but have to wait for the aftermath of Bertha to fade first. Until then I'll get reacquainted with a famous figure along the coast that has come to symbolise islandness. I can walk to the old fishing village of Lower Largo along the beach.

He shields his ferocious gaze across the sea. He looks past the slipway towards a shore made of cakes of red sandstone holding rockpools wherein upturned crabs like the cuticles of little drowned fingernails are hunted by gulls and fish flap under bladderwrack. To see the sea, his stare must laser through houses in the way. He's bearded, dressed in goatskins, holding a musket and he stands astride the lintels of two front doors on Main Street. He looked nothing like this when he left Lower Largo aged seventeen in 1693. There is a stone plaque beneath him:

IN MEMORY OF ALEXANDER SELKIRK
MARINER, THE ORIGINAL OF ROBINSON CRUSOE WHO
LIVED ON THE ISLAND OF JUAN FERNANDEZ IN COMPLETE
SOLITUDE FOR FOUR YEARS AND FOUR MONTHS. HE DIED
1723 LEUITENANT OF H.M.S WEYMOUTH AGED 47 YEARS.
THIS STATUE IS ERECTED BY DAVID GILLIES,
NET MANUFACTURER, ON THE SITE OF THE
COTTAGE IN WHICH SELKIRK WAS BORN.

Selkirk would have torn around this village like Alex the pit bull off his lead. The tanner's son was a wild boy with a temper and a healthy disrespect for authority; these attributes got him in trouble with the kirk and the law but served him well as a buccaneer when he skipped his court appearance, joining a ship with the king's licence to plunder Spanish galleons in the New World. In 1704, having sailed around Cape Horn as second-in-command of the *Cinque Ports*, he became convinced the ship was not seaworthy and would sink in the next storm. He demanded to be put ashore while re-provisioning the ship on the Juan Fernández archipelago 420 miles off the coast of Chile. Captain Stradling was glad to be rid of him and had Selkirk rowed ashore to Más a Tierra island with some essential survival kit and nothing more. Selkirk changed his mind at the last minute but Stradling wouldn't have him back and so he became the most famous castaway in history.

Selkirk was right. The *Cinque Ports* was hit by a storm and the crew were either drowned or captured to endure the terrors of a Peruvian gaol. Selkirk toughed it out on the island: hunting goats, using his tanner's skills to make clothes from their hides, hiding from Spanish militia pursuing British buccaneers to save his own. Most of all, Selkirk was on watch, climbing to his lookout high above Cumberland Bay and scanning the sea for salvation just as he once looked from Largo Law, the pap-shaped hill the boy Alex ran up to cast his dreams of sin and adventure out to sea like gannets. For four years and four months on Más a Tierra, he set his ferocious gaze on the Pacific and sent his prayers over the horizon with the albatross until, on 2 February 1709, he was rescued by a privateer called the *Duke*. A brass plaque was placed at El Mirador de Selkirk, Selkirk's lookout, by the crew of HMS *Topaze* in 1863. The plaque established two things. Firstly: in 150 years, the military and commercial power of Empire had reached the last remote places on Earth. Secondly, the Empire had no need of Selkirks. It wanted an English hero of moral and social standing, with a slave, to be a castaway in the Caribbean whose islands were generating English wealth. It wanted a fictional, anglicised Selkirk for the first-ever English novel, life as literature. The Empire wanted Daniel Defoe's Robinson Crusoe. By 1966, in a bid to stimulate tourism, the president of Chile changed the name of Más a Tierra to Robinson Crusoe Island.

I arrived on Robinson Crusoe Island by plane from the old Chilean port city of Valparaiso. I had been reporting on an international conference in Valparaiso about the biodiversity emergency on the Juan Fernández Islands when I was invited to accompany a handful of journalists and scientists to see the islands for themselves. The bright red poppies and yellow sunflowers growing out of bare earth around the little runway created an unreal, unfinished atmosphere on that part of the island which still holds the trauma of recent seismic events. Arguably, human history brought worse traumas. Trouble first came to these islands in 1540 when their discoverer, Juan Fernández, dropped off four goats to provide food for future mariners. Subsequent overgrazing by goats, cattle, sheep, horses and rabbits led to irreversible erosion. Rats and mice jumped ship to become predators of birds and gnawers of rare plants. New plants arrived with pirates, garrisons and migrants and flowers skipped over garden fences to colonise disturbed land and oust vegetation which had evolved over 4 million years. The native Magellan thrush spreads non-native seeds far and wide. The astonishingly beautiful Juan Fernández firecrown, a little ginger hummingbird adapted to the pristine forest and one of the rarest birds in the world, is forced to find food in the village gardens where it is vulnerable to attack by domestic cats. Legend has it that South American coati – cat-sized mongoose or racoon-like mammals – were released to provide more wildlife interest when the islands were designated a national park in the 1930s only to become predators of the Juan Fernández petrel, a seabird which nests in burrows here and nowhere else. In the 1960s someone thought the European blackberry would make a good hedge. Now bramble grows into enormous thickets, waves of it sweeping across hillsides, smothering endemic trees. The unique ecology of the Juan Fernández Islands faces catastrophe.

Shoot the goats, poison the rats, grub out the bramble: the consensus among conservation scientists is for drastic action. Conservationists from New Zealand have had success in getting rid of invasive species such as rats and cats on Tiritiri Matangi Island among others and are confident they can do the same in the Juan Fernández archipelago. Many in the local community also back these measures: 'We must act now,' says one islander, 'our islands are dying.' Like Alexander Selkirk, conservationists dream of deliverance, too. 'The important thing about this biodiversity is that it has a meaning for itself but it's up to us to take care of it,' says Ivan Julio Leiva Silva who, as director of the Juan Fernández National Park, has been struggling with its problems for fifteen years. It seems tragically unlikely to me. The notion of biodiversity having meaning for itself and intrinsic value in Nature is something I feel acutely while walking among exquisite ferns and flowering trees endemic to the Juan Fernández Islands, a forest that grows nowhere else on Earth. If I could invent an island ecology that reflected my own temperate fantasy forest, it would look like this. But it's broken. The Juan Fernández archipelago is as biologically important as the Galapagos Islands, yet that alone is not enough to save it. The ecological consequences of human travel and colonisation are tragedies repeated all over the world. I was invited here as an advocate, and I am, but in environmental terms my own presence on Robinson Crusoe Island is part of its problem. The corrosive effects of civilisation are felt most acutely on isolated islands. I think of Wenlock Edge as an island: a sinuous reef under woods and fields holding on to what remains of its wild secrets against the greedy scratchings of civilisation.

In the eighteenth-century English imagination, Selkirk became an island, subjected to the horror of isolation in William Cowper's poem 'The Solitude of Alexander Selkirk', which begins with the much repeated, ironic line: *I am monarch of all I survey*.

> My right there is none to dispute,
> From the centre all round to the sea,
> I am lord of the fowl and the brute.

That will to power over Nature, whether from the feudal right of lordly dominance or the more modern managerial role of stewardship, emerges from ecophobia and the fear of being besieged by wild Nature, being a castaway. After his rescue, Alexander Selkirk took to buccaneering with enthusiasm and on his return achieved celebrity status. But he couldn't settle. He returned to Lower Largo, ran off with a sixteen-year-old dairymaid, went to London, took up with a widowed innkeeper in Plymouth, got into trouble and skipped off again. Yellow fever caught up with Selkirk on 13 December 1723 on HMS *Weymouth* off the coast of Africa.

At the age of forty-seven he was buried at sea. Whatever power we may imagine we have, Nature's is greater. Just a couple of months after I visited Robinson Crusoe Island, an earthquake in Chile sent a tidal wave that destroyed much of its coastal area including the village of San Juan Bautista, killing many people, some of whom I'd met. Through the cloud, the little Juan Fernández firecrowns sang in the last 250 hectares of remaining pristine forest without knowing how critically their days are numbered.

I have an island of my own. Perhaps it's Wenlock Edge but perhaps it's somewhere out to sea, I don't know where it is. I keep looking. The Alexander Selkirk-as-Robinson Crusoe statue in Lower Largo found his island; he was saved from it but fought against salvation until the sea took him. Lost, he spies fair weather across the Firth of Forth and that means I can catch the tourist boat, the *Princess of May*, from the middle pier opposite the Scottish Fisheries Museum in Anstruther. Having had the privilege of visiting the Juan Fernández Islands, I want to see the island that drew Alexander Selkirk out to sea, the Isle of May, and make the reverse connection as if this were an act of return.

The sea is quite calm and as the houses on shore get smaller, thistledown like fifty-legged glass spiders drifts over the water towards the Isle of May, a green reclining figure, strangely close. Sitting on the sea are groups of guillemots and a few rare Manx shearwaters. Gannets turn on the black tips of their long white wings like compasses on pilot charts. Approaching the isle feels like something from a sixties film: nostalgic, charmingly bucolic with just a hint of licentiousness and malice. Circling the island on its eastern side, a silent crowd of grey seals stick their soft-eyed dog faces out of the water to watch the boat. They are expecting something to happen and, not disappointed exactly, they are resigned to their visitors being *unexciting*. Grey seals are gathering here from around the North Sea coast to pup and mate; there will be 4,000 of them this autumn. The Isle of May is a midwife island: thousands of puffins, razorbills, guillemots, shags, Arctic terns and kittiwakes come to give birth and raise their young as well as grey seals. There has been a bird observatory here since 1934 and since 1956 this island has been a National Nature Reserve, one of the most important breeding sites for seabirds and seals in the North Sea and protected for the kind of secular Nature worship observed through binocular and camera lenses. In another time, one when the Isle of May was also a reserve for smugglers, I imagine young Alex Selkirk here, pulling puffin chicks from burrows, climbing cliffs to steal razorbill eggs from fingertip ledges, skinning seals and harpooning porpoise and minke whale as seafaring people had done for centuries. Wherever there's life, there's a tradition of taking it.

Such a fate befell those who lie under a pile of stones. On the Isle of May or Maia – whose name originates from Pictish tribes or a Gothic word for green isle – there is evidence of thousands of years of human occupation, the most potent of which is a burial cairn made of over a million fist-sized stones. Although begun in prehistory, the legend of the sacred isle was reshaped during the Dark Ages when Ethernan, a Christian holy man of Irish or maybe Hungarian descent but an important figure in Pictish Christianity, came with monks in the middle of the ninth century to establish a religious community. In 875, the Vikings raided and slaughtered them all; the legendary death toll was 6,600. Ethernan – whose name was Latinised to Adrian – and the monks were interred in the cairn of stones making it a holy shrine. The religious colony was abandoned until the mid-twelfth century when a small monastery was re-established, dedicated to the Virgin Mary and Ethernan. However, this too was harassed by Orkney Vikings until it passed to the English. Under occupation, the Isle of May monastery became a symbol of Scottish identity in the Wars of Scottish Independence until it was destroyed by the English. A chapel was rebuilt to St Adrian which stood until the Reformation when the island was sold and the smugglers moved in. The last inhabitant died in 1730 and the Isle of May was left to the lighthouses and 50,000 scarts, dun turs, gulls, scouts and kittiwakes. During the Middle Ages, the island was visited by half a million pilgrims seeking divine intercession from St Adrian – the anglicised version of Ethernan – and each picked a stone from the shore and placed it on the cairn; each stone represented a place in heaven. According to a medieval quote on the information board in the chapel ruins: *Holy men expelled demons and wild beasts from the Island of May.*

What demons? What wild beasts? May could have had great auks – which looked like penguins, relatives of guillemots and razorbills – and sea eagles, both of which became extinct. Had someone put wolves there; were there walruses, visiting orcas; shamans calling up spirits of the old religions? Perhaps the birds were banished. Even at the tail end of the breeding season when most of the chicks hatched on the isle have fledged and flown, the sound of seabird society calling, scolding, demanding, alarming, squabbling, pleading, leaving and arriving, is so loud and constant that it sets up an aural edge the mind can tip over. During the height of the breeding season these rituals of sound are overwhelming. I've been on the Farne Islands off Northumbria, which are similar to this, and the seabird sound is intense. Together with dive-bombing terns drawing blood and crapping on visitors, the experience can be scary and disorientating. Was Ethernan, like Selkirk, 'monarch of all he surveyed'? Did he have the power to drive the wildlife away or were there other things which cannot even be spoken about now, inhabiting or haunting the Isle of May that he exorcised? Whatever power the devout had over their solitude it could not control the Vikings. We have come to think of the Norse as bloodthirsty barbarians who slaughtered innocent Christians for kicks and stole their sacraments as trophies – actually, the English also did this – but I wonder if that's what happened here. Suppose the Vikings were outraged by the desecration of this sacred place by Christians. Perhaps what the Christian holy men thought of as demons, the Viking holy men held as sacred beings whose expulsion demanded retribution.

A tattered and exhausted pilgrim in white, red and black: a red admiral butterfly settles on the ruined tower. It has nowhere to go now and if a bird doesn't eat it, its husk will crumble into the island's duff, along with the saints and sinners, to become the purple of heather bells. The great black-backed gulls leave their dead stiff and folded on the ground to be eaten by mice and stand on rocks either side of a narrow path regarding me with something between disdain and pathological hatred. *Error . . . error . . . error*, they call. They will stay here, a garrison waiting for any opportunity to satisfy its fearsome appetite as a matter of entitlement.

The Arctic terns, called *stearnan* in Gaelic, have other plans. They are still feeding a late brood, appearing out of the sky like white swallows with black caps and silvery fish in their bright-red beaks. Their demanding chicks, hiding under little wooden bird houses made to protect them from the raiding gulls, have only a couple of weeks to fledge before they begin the longest migration of any bird on Earth. These terns are at the southern edge of their Arctic breeding range and juveniles may travel east, first to Scandinavia and the Baltic but the main direction of movement will be southwards, down the west coast of Europe, along the west coast of Africa and beyond the Cape to the food-rich pack ice of Antarctica. They spread out and some of those fledged here may spend two years circumnavigating Antarctica before migrating north. In small bands of a dozen, at high altitude across open oceans, the movements of *stearnan* are still a mystery: how many of the American and Siberian birds move through Britain on their way south, whether all those born on the isle will return here, when they achieve breeding age and where they range, is unclear. A 20,000-mile round trip to Antarctica is astounding but that they will travel further than Alexander Selkirk's epic round-the-world journey every year of their lives, beggars belief. Unimpressed, the terns chicker and swear at intruders, less inclined to direct violence now, fighting against time to get their precocious children into the air. Towards the end of August there is a change in the light, a signal to the *stearnan* to seek the sun. It also signals the next wave of migration is coming soon: Nordic thrushes – redwings and fieldfares – will plunder Britain for the blood-red berries of rowan, holly, hawthorn and yew. The great sky-roads of geese and swans will open and arrowheaded skeins will come honking, refugees from the endless dark of Arctic winter. I stand on the Isle of May next to the fog warning station and peer like Selkirk into the grey. I have an island of my own somewhere and I keep looking for it.

HARE

Waking up in a hostel dormitory with sixteen other people, I try to become invisible as I pack up and sneak out into the cobbled square under the shadow of a horse chestnut tree, quiet and strangely birdless. The Skärgården ferry leaves Stockholm at 8.30. The opportunity to go on a writing retreat to a Swedish island, to follow the trajectory of my gaze across the North Sea into the heart of those who raided the Isle of May and shaped much of British history, is, like the serendipity which linked the Juan Fernández Islands to the Isle of May through Alexander Selkirk, an irresistible act of return. The journey takes over three hours, pinballing between stops at islands with pretty houses in the archipelago. Overhead, a mustering of black storks flies west; an osprey materialises, soaring prospectively then vanishes and the huge dark form of a sea eagle flies out of myth, shaking the sky. Finnhamn – where Finns once had a harbour settlement – is a holiday island in the Skärgården, the Stockholm archipelago. It has a hostel, a cafe-restaurant, a shop, wooden chalets, campsites and boat moorings. There's a farm and some meadows but the rest is woodland and bare rock. The cafe plays Clapton's 'Cocaine' for a well-heeled, ageing clientele at the tail end of the holiday season and I think about how the most feared warrior cult in Europe became one of its most liberal societies.

However, the Scandinavian link between water and wood remains strong, shaping the being-in-Nature fantasy, feeding the Viking legends and taking shape in these powerfully alluring islands. As if to divert me from thinking about this, the most extraordinary butterfly appears in dapple shade under oaks and pines. A Camberwell beauty: purply-brown drapery with sapphire dots and cream-yellow edges like theatre curtains – a beautiful and very rare visitor to Britain and one I've only seen as dead specimens and illustrations – is feeding in dried dog shit on the path. It is a talisman I would have chased to the ends of the Earth if it had appeared in my childhood. It has a totemic value to a tribe of acquisitive naturalists I belonged to in another part of my life and yet I still feel the surge of excitement. The butterfly, in all its sordid glory, subverts those stories of species, taxonomy and scientific objectivity we tell about Nature now: some wild individuals appear as islands of themselves, surrounded by our presumptions and expectations of them.

Before dusk, I leave the wooden shed called *Ensamheten*, the Lonely Place, I'm staying in for a week to do some writing, and walk on to the slabs of bare rock between pines behind it. These glacier-smoothed and scarred platforms of grey granite bristle with miniature woods of silver-grey *Cladonia* lichen called reindeer moss, a true Arctic plant which still clings to the legacy of the Ice Age in parts of Britain and is used in Scandinavia in the manufacture of alcohol. The open slabs have fault lines and cracks wherein grow the most exquisite trees. Each gaunt, twisted, stunted pine or cluster of pines has a unique character. They may not be valued here as such but they are the wild models for what in Chinese culture became penjing, the practice of growing trees in pots to be sculpted by pruning, trimming and wiring into living, three-dimensional poetry, a re-creation of magical landscapes in Taoist mysticism which, influenced by Chan Buddhism, became the more formal Zen art of Japanese bonsai. These pines are stressed, their roots struggling through tiny cracks for water and nutrients, exposed to high winds, covered in snow and enduring freezing winters; survival is tenuous, growth is slow and sometimes negligible for centuries. There is an aesthetic in these charismatic dwarfs that carries a spiritual dimension – an ideal of the forest-mountain miniaturised, an island floating free from the everyday world, a suffering that transcends mortality. In the West, the desire for these stunted, characterful trees in rockeries and suburban gardens is a way in which idealised Nature enters culture and these aberrant forms create an enchanted space in which scale is reduced while the imagination is expanded. I have spent a lot of time in the company of such trees in the wild and in nurseries in Britain and the United States and I can see the attraction for dwarf conifer enthusiasts. There is something achingly perfect about these trees which synthesises wood and stone, great age and unique character; a kind of wind-through-pines poem written by the great Chinese poet Li Po made real. On the other side of the world, he was writing in what we call the Dark Ages, at the same time Vikings were rowing their longships from these islands towards the west, facing their future with sharpened axes. Odin sends one of his ravens to spy on Finnhamn and it *kronks* overhead.

A sudden drumming: not loud but startling in its reverberation through me. I turn to see a hare. She has run a short distance over bare rock, drumming an alarm with her powerful back legs. Now she crouches with her head cocked, watching me. I have felt this gaze before.

I was on Orford Ness, the longest vegetated shingle spit in Europe. It runs for over 10 miles along the Suffolk coast from Aldeburgh to Shingle Street, north of the port of Felixstowe. 'Ness' means 'nose' and it's a snout of land nudging into the North Sea on one side and harbouring the estuary of the Rivers Alde and Ore on the other. Between the sea and the river are brackish lagoons, wet grasslands, reed beds, mudflats, grazing marsh and miles of stony shingle ridges. I was staying here on my own in the old buildings which once belonged to the Ministry of Defence and now the National Trust. The distinctive elements of Orford Ness seemed a simple trinity: stone, water and sky. But there was something in the way these elements sounded to me: the way the sea smacked against the shingle; the way the light reflected on the stones and pools; the way the wind cried over the flat ground. This was far from simple. There was something else in the aural landscape of Orford Ness, some feral power beyond its history of secret military weapons testing, something disturbing yet seductive. One evening I watched as a curlew flew into a flame and purple sunset. On the edge of a lagoon, a pair of spoonbills – tall, mysterious and white – watched me intently.

After a day's wandering and a constant battering from the wind, I returned to the barracks to cook something to eat and drink wine. At midnight I was very uneasy. Perhaps it was the wine, the long day and the strangeness of the place but I had an ominous feeling that something was about to happen. The silence in the barracks became oppressive. I opened the door onto the street. There in the centre of the pool of light was a hare. It had a strange crouching gait. It cocked its head to one side and stared at me as it almost crawled by into the darkness. The moon was rising above the sound of waves on shingle, the sea polishing and positioning each pebble meticulously into its own secret place. Still spooked by the hare, it occurred to me that I walked that road of stones between sea and sky in the pointless round and round of nowhere. Sorrow was a ripple closing on the moon as white birds scattered. One day I would follow them across the waves.

The name *hare*, from the Old Nordic *heri*, is the same, although pronounced differently, in Swedish and English. The hare watches for a moment and then, through a powerfully muscular twist with something grotesque about it, she runs off across the stone with its archipelago of wonderful trees. The hare's path leads into the heart of the island. It is the opposite response to Selkirk who constantly looked away from his island prison, his life at first given context by what he was cast away from. His salvation would come from the sea, as he had. But, gradually, the island absorbed him. It was only on Más a Tierra that he felt peace, a physical and spiritual well-being that he'd never felt before and never felt again. The hare is that wild spirit which in her drumming becomes the sounding of stone; her gaze asks a question of existence and her path leads to the fugitive heart of the isle which vanishes before it can be defined.

I wonder if any of these old trees grew here during Viking times; it is certainly an ancient forest that goes back to the end of the Ice Age and, south of the Caledonian forest in the Highlands of Scotland, such wild pine woods have not been seen for thousands of years in Britain. I imagine they are similar to the forests that lie submerged under Cardigan Bay in Wales. I climb one of a group of seven pines, the tallest being only 15 feet high. I bear the scratches, risk the snapped branches and breathe the scent of resin. This must be the highest point on this side of the island, a lookout towards the sea. The sun is easing into the west behind other wooded islands and its glow strikes the pines, lights them up: orange, animal, a light filling the tree inside, then leaving it. I cast a shadow across the rock: that old dark scarecrow leans into green needles. And then, in a momentary fog, the pine and I become a brocken spectre – a shadowy ghost with a halo of red, orange, gold as the low sun projects our image against the antisolar point in the fog. It lifts in seconds under a sky with pale sweeps of cloud and jittery house martins against the sun glittering the sea. I slide down a rock slope, marked 2013 in white paint, to the water's edge. This is the Baltic: *slop*, *ploop*, *boop*, a shuffle of waves against stone; I slide in up to my knees in the same sea my dad walked on when it was frozen back in 1945 while he was stationed in

Schleswig-Holstein during the war. The water is cool, brackish and without tide, unlike any sea I've known.

There is a deeper rumbling like rocks underwater but it's coming from an inlet where a boat has pushed a pontoon in and there's a clattering of hooves on its deck: cows, black with short horns, ten of them. The farmer is standing on a picnic table on the shore, hauling the pontoon in with a long rope. Then she climbs back to move the metal gates penning the cattle in. They're nervous and start to jostle. She has words of encouragement and some run ashore but two bullocks panic, rearing up on the railings. If they jump overboard they'll be trapped in the water between the rocks and the pontoon. The dog barks. The farmer screams at them and pushes one back off the railings. He runs ashore bucking and kicking like a rodeo bull.

The farmer gives a call: it begins as a shout, then jumps pitch like a yodel to a soprano note which sounds like *cooooooooooow*. It is a wild singing that cuts through the clear sunset air over the island. It sounds like an exclamation of passion for the land and for the beast, for strength and for joy. Where did it come from? For centuries farmers have practised transhumance, where cattle are taken out to graze on islands in the winter and in more recent years in Sweden this has been revived for the conservation of grasslands. The farmer's is a personal adaptation of the pastoral yell that, like the hunter's howl, carries the voice so well over long distances. However, it is more powerful than a telecommunications link with other isolated people scattered across islands or mountains. It is a song that names the land it sings. There is something ancient about this sound in this forest that plants a truth in it. It gives voice to a language far older than those we speak now and belongs to a place which may also have changed beyond our comprehension. The song reverberates, like the hare's drumming, around the core of the island. It creates, in a ritual act, a peal of stillness that is not sentimental, but draws into itself a listening, a recognition and an inner response. The cows moo back; black cattle in the night.

BRAN GOESGOCH

The poet R.S. Thomas told me that when you arrive at a remote railway station at night and all you hear is the sound of running water, you know you're in Wales. Back from the Skärgården, I follow a line of memory to the western shore where for me there is another act of returning to an island. Here, I am searching for an island within an island, a secret wild on the edge of the sea I feel closest to.

Llwyngwril is just such a railway station that Thomas would have loved and the River Gwril is in fine voice. Brown as beer and roiling from rain in the mountains, the river is named after Gwril the giant who drinks tonight in the Garth up on the main road. He's too big to get back in his council pickup, too drunk to drive, he stares at the newcomers and chuckles mischievously, swears in English but a wild Welsh poetry tumbles from him, out of the pub, under the bridge, all the way past the holiday homes, along the common where the gypsies camped and the smithy where they had their horses shod, past the caravan site and the railway station, through the shingle and into the sea.

The sea breathes Gwril's old sentences, whips his liquid consonants to froth, rolls up his hisses and sighs and the sly pauses wherein danger lies, opening them out into the longshore drift of Cardigan Bay.

A pair of choughs drops out of the sky over the old church of St Celynnin. *Ch-owe . . . chowe, chowe, chowe . . .* they yell into the clear bright air over cliffs. The sound they make becomes their name, when the 'ough' in chough is rhymed with *bough* not *cough*. In Welsh they're called Bran goesgoch, red-legged crow, and so they are. With downturned red beaks, all black with blue and green iridescence and wide fingered wings, choughs are emblematic birds. They are always a thrill to see and the last I saw were on Islay in Scotland's Inner Hebrides.

On Islay, between Ardnave Point and Nave Island, grey seals patrolled the straits of Na Badagan with a gaggle of moulting greylag geese. Behind the ruined chapel were cliffs where peregrine falcons nested. A buzzard traced a thermal above rabbit-scurrying dunes. There were lawns of blue speedwell or yellow cinquefoil and in wet flushes redshank and lapwing stepped with a nervousness that at times overcame them and they launched into the air, calling plaintively before settling again, in their own unsettled way. And all the while, Islay's larks powered skyward, propelled by song. Suddenly, from the corner of my eye, I saw something black lob over a dune. As I followed it, two umbrella-handle heads poked from the marram grass and shouted a challenge. They were a pair of young choughs, their beaks still orange instead of red, and they were watching me intently. Then two adult birds swerved through the air and landed nearby. Their glossy black plumage, pillar-box red curved beaks and legs give them a heraldic elegance. In fact choughs appear on the Cornish coat of arms and there's a legend that King Arthur's soul migrated into a chough so that he would not die. Watching them close up – the airy grace of their flight, the swaggering walk, the tribal black and red costume – it's easy to imagine the traffic of spirits between ancient heroes and choughs. They're iconic birds of the western sea cliffs and hills, a tribe of crows that share that dark yet playful corvid intelligence but have evolved a lightness of being. *Ch-owe* . . . it's a sharp, ominous exclamation but with a lyrical twist from a living mythology tied to the margins of the western lands, to the sun and the sea.

Back at Cardigan Bay, the chattering of choughs over this ancient Welsh churchyard may, like the Arthurian legend, tell stories about other transmigrating souls. This church is dedicated to Celynnin who, in legend, was a son of the prince of Llys Helig, the mythical drowned land on the North Wales coast, with tribal connections to the rulers of Maes Gwyddno, the plain which ran from Bardsey Island to Pembrokeshire out there under Cardigan Bay, lands which medieval manuscripts refer to as 'the Kingdoms which the sea destroyed'. Inside the church, on Dark Age footings torched by Vikings and rebuilt in the Middle Ages, are 500-year-old frescos. These are fragments of religious texts except for the surviving memento mori, a painted skeleton holding a scythe and what may be a burning torch. The skeleton is headless but has a skull and crossbones between its feet. In the church porch, there's a grey beach stone built into the wall below the squint, hollowed to make a water stoup.

At the entrance, by the path, is a flat stone on which is carved WAW 1774–1800. This is the grave of Abram Wood,

King of the Gypsies. Wood's grave is a kind of threshold. I have to walk over the King of the Gypsies into the graveyard with its beautifully lettered headstones in English and Welsh, which begin with the word UNDERNEATH. Colonies of *Cladonia* lichen, reindeer moss, grow on the stones and surrounding walls. The lychgate opens onto fields which rise up the hill behind to the Iron Age fort on top. The west is a great sweep of Cardigan Bay looking along the Llyn Peninsula to *Ynys Enlli*, Bardsey Island: home to grey seals, Manx shearwaters, 20,000 saints and *Bran goesgoch*. *Ch-owe . . . chowe, chowe, chowe . . .* yell Celynnin and Abram Wood above the train to Tywyn. Underneath a bright, chough-flown sky, the past and those who lived in it lives still. Underneath the sea, a forest stirs.

Drunk last night, Gwril punched a hole through the shingle bank and the river opened a new channel to the sea. At low tide the next day, I walk through new mountain water riffling across the few hundred yards of stony beach down to open sand. Cwtiad Torchog, the ringed plover, flies from a smooth grey rock banded with white quartzite. There are scattered colonies of little brown blades, brittle crystalline algae looking like plumage and outcrops of maerl on clay lumps. The waves are slight, whispering. A few gulls and meadow pipits lift and fall around the rockpools, otherwise there is little movement. The journey back up the beach is difficult, stones green with gutweed are slippery, balance is unsteady. Towards the shingle bank I find a more open patch to pause and look inland. This tumble of stones that makes the beach comes from glacial moraines higher up. There are raised beaches, a coastline perched in the hills. The tideline has changed many times between ice ages and much of this debris was dumped here from Northern Ireland when the last glacier melted. For thousands of years the ice sheet locked up so much water that the sea level fell and Britain was not an island but joined to the continent and to Ireland; mammoth teeth, lion bones, stone axes and arrowheads are constantly washed up from lands under the sea. From 19,000 years ago the sea level has risen 120 metres, sometimes at the rate of 1 metre a century but sometimes jumping twice that. By 6,000 years ago Britain was an island again.

I look down to what my feet are standing on in the gap between stones. It's a bed of clay with what looks like a lump of wood sticking out. It is and there are others, root ends, bits of root or branch, a few more substantial pieces. This is not a timber dump, this is the remains of a forest. This is what I wanted to find earlier in the year but couldn't get to because of the storm and high tide. I really hadn't expected to find it here. The more I look the more I see. This forest, over 6,000 years old, stretches out into Cardigan Bay to become the legendary Maes Gwyddno or Cantre'r Gwaelod, the *bottom hundred under the sea*. In the stories, all it took was a night of drunkenness to neglect the sea defences and the land was flooded and lost forever. This could be a modern morality tale. Our civilisation, drunk on its achievements, drunk to forget its fear of Nature, neglects its responsibilities. As climate change takes greater hold, the seas rise inexorably.

I see another open area in the stones about 50 feet long and 15 feet wide covered in 6 inches of water. Shrimp and small fish dart over the shining clay and there are long pine roots embedded in it and a 6-foot branch bearing what appears to be axe marks cut like runes. I walk carefully. This is the forest like that on the island of Finnhamn in Sweden: pine, birch, aspen but inhabited by animals and people I can barely imagine. This forest, due to climate change many thousands of years ago, died off and has become covered in peat and then covered again by sand and pebbles of the longshore drift of Cardigan Bay. This year's storms stripped the layers away in some places and here between stones I look down to see that I'm standing on a pine stump, its roots radiating out in all directions like the cardinal points of a compass. I don't know how old it is; according to carbon dating of similar timbers exposed in the area, it may be from 1740–1420 BC or even further back to the Mesolithic, 7000 BC. This one tree is an isle, another storm will bury it again. The revelation is humbling and exciting and I can imagine the forest it belonged to. I feel this pine to be like one of those beautifully characterful individuals I saw on Finnhamn and a reminder that, like Robinson Crusoe Island, a forest is a living community of unique things. I cannot think of it as dead, only transformed, suspended, waiting. Now, in this fleeting moment and by accident or serendipity, I too am part of that community. This is a numinous moment of connection with the deep past which brings it into the present. The story of being here in this secret island forest lost in a changing world appears to me as a fable for the future.

A group of teenagers walks along the shingle bank, laughing and joking. I wonder what they will feel about climate change and sea-level rise and how they will explain it to their children and how their children will wonder at the drowned lands and lost islands. The kids walk over to an old man with a beard sitting on a bench above the beach. He's been watching my exploration of the forest fragment and probably knows far more about it than I do. Now he's watching the sun set in the gap between Bardsey Island (Ynys Enlli) and the Llyn peninsula. One of the girls says to him, 'My friend says that when the sun goes into the sea the water boils, is that true?' The old man smiles and says, 'Only at weekends.'

9.
BODY

The physical structure whether dead or alive; the main part of a thing or aggregate association; society of things; a quantity, being, person, mass; a full substantial quality.

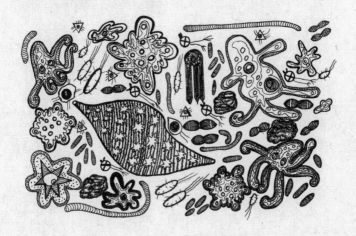

FOUR-SPOT ORB WEAVER

Fog lifts from the spider fields. As sunlight floods the hollow it is trapped in millions of dew pearls threaded on gossamer. Wrens chip away at the morning with sharp stones of sound. Between every thistle, ragwort and grass stem is slung a spider's web. There are thousands of them across the field; each web a unique device. Together the spiders have rigged the world as far as the eye can see; the trap is sprung.

Along the lane are fruity puddles of crab-apple and damson windfalls; there are swags of scarlet honeysuckle and bryony berries in the hedge, late blackberries, dark-blue sloes, red hips, haws and holly berries. A good supply of wild seeds and fruits means a high breeding population of mice and voles next year, which means more successful broods of barn owls and tawny owls next spring. Plenty of foliage for the caterpillars and flowers for the adults is good for the moth population, which in turn is food for bats that have returned to their breeding roosts now the sun's up. Well-fed bats in good condition will hibernate through winter.

All this is a small part of a huge ecological web spun across the autumnal landscape and in the middle of it sits the spider, a symbol for all those myriad lives which lash this story together. I imagine a symbolic spider: a four-spot orb weaver; she has a huge orb, a bun-shaped hat of an abdomen in subtle brown shades with four very conspicuous white spots, one each for Earth, Fire, Air and Water; she has tied her victims up in silk as mementos, killed her lover and is bursting with 900 eggs.

We may not know the world as our ancestors did; our urbanised lives may not follow the rhythm of the changing seasons and the seasons themselves have had their rhythm broken by our business. But our senses are still hitched to natural phenomena and, like the gossamer threads slung by nocturnal orb spiders in autumn, they twitch with meaning and significance when some fleeting sight, sound, smell, taste, touch or thought trips them. This sensory vibration is keenest in the dark, the fog or in that liminal state emerging into day when spiders weave with light. Even if we are not foraging for wild food, we are still eager collectors of wild stimulants: the changing leaf pigments, the sharp chill of morning air, the mysterious mood-altering fogs. We seek experience, capturing a natural aesthetic from the world around us and like the orb spider, wrapping it up in memory, gorging on inspiration. Fog lingers on the hills; it traps me in a pool of glittering sunlight opening to the sky.

When I talk about being in a hollow on Wenlock Edge or looking into rockpools on a Welsh beach or watching a seabird colony on a Scottish island, who or what am I talking about? When I include myself in my stories about places and the things that live there, I am doing so as a participant not as a detached observer. I may be *present* in these places, and they become my experience, but my experience of them is not their experience of me. It is arrogant of me to presume my presence has any effect on what I experience; the spiders, limpets and birds carry on in the same way they would without me. Sometimes I do have a connection, a contact with other living beings which, however fleeting, is a moment I cherish, even if such sentiments are not reciprocated by the wildlife. Being trapped by 10,000 glittering spiders' webs under an autumnal sky can be a transformative experience and when Nature has such a profound effect I struggle to describe it. Language becomes inadequate and terms such as 'sacred' or 'magical' have lost their potency and can be as clichéd as 'stunning', 'incredible' or 'fantastic'. I struggle with the intimate language I use to describe Nature, trying not to make my emotional responses appear trite or twee. Sometimes this works well, and sometimes not, and so to avoid the risk of embarrassing purple there's a counter tendency to stand back, as a detached scientific observer or journalist might do, and recount the experience as if there were no emotional connection. This is an abdication of responsibility: bearing witness, being truthful, requires emotional honesty.

The language problem is not confined to positive experiences of Nature. There can be a very thin line between awe and fear and the numinous can become the disastrous through terror or distress. When I read newspaper headlines referring to hurricanes as *monsters*, volcanoes as *Nature's wrath* or floods *claiming victims* I have to appreciate that these descriptions are how Nature is experienced by those caught in such events. Both extremes of love and fear give rise to notions of Nature's intentionality, good and evil. Perhaps the projection of human imagination onto Nature interprets it in these ways, but although we may now consider the personification of Nature unreasonable – Mother Nature, Nature's wrath or Nature's bounty – this is the way we talk about our experience of Nature; it feels reasonable. Of course the normal way of living rarely touches these extremes and is a kind of coming to terms with Nature's crushing indifference, illuminated by momentary connections which bring other lives and places into consciousness.

Consciousness has to be conscious of something and my own consciousness may be conscious of something that has no consciousness of me and yet my body may be a direct and almost certainly an indirect threat to the wildlife and wild places I seek. I often hear people talk about human beings as a cancer, destroyers and polluters of the Earth as if we were aliens, somehow detached from Nature. I think they're talking about the human ego, which developed from an aggressive-defensive response to ecophobia. A fear of Nature, including human nature, sets the ego apart as sometimes guardian, sometimes avenging angel. My body, however, reveals a very different story of interdependence and community.

One of the most astonishing things I've learned in recent years is that only one in ten cells of my body is human. According to the Human Microbiome Project, set up in 2008 to identify and catalogue microbes in the human body, my microbiome is not just the complement of bacteria, fungi, protozoa and viruses living in me but their genetic capabilities, too. Of the entire DNA in my body, 90 per cent of it is carried by microbes in my gut alone, so only 10 per cent of my genetic material is human. I am a bag of germs. In my large intestine are a thousand species of bacteria which make up 10 to the power 14 per gram of the material in there, 100 million trillion individual lives. Not just in my gut – there are microbes up my nose, down my throat, in my mouth, over my skin, even inside my brain. Without them I could not digest food, breathe, sustain an immune system and, perhaps most controversially, think. I carry so many microbes around in my body that I depend on for my very existence. When I walk through a wood, order a drink at the bar, go to the public lavatory, so do my microbes; some of them will leave and others which lived in someone or something else will join me. There will be readjustments as cells die, migrate, reproduce. I travel from the spider fields where I am attached by gossamer threads to thousands of creatures to London where I walk in an invisible smog of microbes that become part of me with every breath and touch. In neither of these places am I actually alone. So what do I mean by *me*?

I peer into a microscope in a laboratory at the top of Guy's Hospital in London. I've come to talk to Professor William Wade, head of the microbiology unit of King's College dental institute about the work he contributes to the Human Microbiome Project. William prepares a slide of dental plaque scraped off teeth. Because of a special dye, the microbes appear as golden dots at first. The more I look, the more I see: a constellation of shining beings, some stationary, some propelling themselves through the liquid. They remind me of the first time I saw fireflies massing in a field enclosed by woods in New England. The swarm of tiny lights hovered, drifted or flew purposefully in the still summer night, thousands and thousands of fireflies completely absorbed in their nuptial flight and one of the most beautiful spectacles I have ever seen. Now I imagine that spectacle happening inside my mouth: a warm dark enclosure where luminous beings swarm. Through the microscope, the microbes drift and dance. They are, as William explains, essential for my health and form quite different communities depending on whether they're living on my teeth, tongue or the soft tissue inside my cheek. He says there's a balance, maintained by brushing my teeth, and to illustrate what happens when this goes awry, he hands me an agar plate with dark lines scribbled over a red substance and asks me to sniff. Uugh! The warm, thick smell is oddly musky, animal and disgusting. It's being produced by bacteria – the culture of dark scribbled lines – feeding on horse blood in agar jelly here but which normally feed on my gums. When there's a population explosion of these bacteria, they produce the most shocking halitosis – a vampire swarm of bad breath.

Medicine will be cast back into the Dark Ages is the current anxiety over bacteria getting out of control. This scare began with 'superbugs' in hospitals resistant to antibiotics and now the reckless use of antibiotics is being blamed for an emerging crisis in which even commonly treatable diseases and infection are becoming resistant. According to a recent article in the *Telegraph*, this is an emergency greater than climate change. The article predicts, based on modelling designed by economists, that unless there's concerted global action to find new treatments and a drastic reduction in the over-prescribing of antibiotics, 300 million people could die by 2050. In this Doomsday scenario, antimicrobial resistance will cause as many deaths as cancer, cholera, diabetes, measles, tetanus, diarrhoeal conditions and all the road traffic accidents in the world combined. Economically, this means the loss of £64 trillion of global productivity in the next thirty-five years, which is equivalent to the UK's GDP each year for a generation.

This is a graphic lesson in the importance of microbial communities. Microbes colonise places in the body and promote populations for the conditions to which they're adapted. Each place – mouth, gut, skin, lungs – has its own community which make up the microbiome. Each community has functions such as the breakdown of nutrients, sustaining natural defences of the immune system and filling the available space to prevent invasions from pathogens and infections. Changes in these communities, such as antibiotics, can have very serious consequences for the body and so a kind of equilibrium within these communities is synonymous with good health. However, not all microbial communities are fixed and there is mobility between them, cross-talk between disjunct sites and over-lapping populations which amounts to communication within and between communities. Mobility of microbes is not restricted to our own body sites but occurs between each other, our children, dogs, cats. My microbes are part of a great cloud of microbes within which exchange is constantly happening.

Herbivores have particular gut communities without which they couldn't break down polysaccharides from the plants in their diet. Carnivores have particular communities for digesting animal fats. Omnivores like me have a mixture of both. Without this combination of gut microbes, which digest and ferment food for me and for other microbes which can't do it themselves, I would not have evolved as a modern human. Trouble in these communities will lead to disbiosis – inflammatory bowel disease, multiple sclerosis, rheumatoid arthritis, depression and other brain conditions. Children get their first dose of microbes at birth from their mothers and thereafter from the environment and the microbe cloud. These beings may have co-evolved with people but they first appeared in the environment as eukaryotic cells – ones with nuclei – 2 billion years ago. I wonder if I should think of myself as part of them rather than imagine they are part of me.

I look out of the humming laboratory's window high up in Guy's Hospital. There is a spectacular view of London's skyline with buildings as modern as the Shard and as old as St Paul's Cathedral. In the spaces within, between and beneath these buildings, human activity is analogous to the body's microbiome. In the city, people are feeding, procreating, making, protecting, communicating, cooperating, destroying, migrating, moving between communities, travelling like neurons in the brain and cells in the spinal cord on cytoplasmic tracks. I imagine all this movement linked by threads that represent the relationships between them.

Yet for me, the analogy for my microbiome and its relationships with the world is not the city. Earth, fire, air, water: the four elements represented by spots on the orb weaver spider are strung together by the lives of countless beings of which I am one community in a community. This fog of being, in which the boundaries and outlines of individuals are blurred by the presence and exchange of millions of microbes, changes what I think of myself as an individual. As I become more aware, I find myself in a misty morning, the sun rising, fog lifting from the spider fields. The trap is sprung.

MAGNIFICENT BRYOZOAN

Various bells strike nine prettily but not quite simultaneously. I get the sense that time in Oxford is arbitrary. But the person I'm visiting is not from this town. For her, nine means nine. I knock on the door of Eastman House and it's opened by the Eastman professor at Balliol College, Oxford University. She – also the distinguished professor of microbial evolution and organelle heredity from the University of Massachusetts, member of the American National Academy of Sciences and recipient of the Presidential Medal of Science – is in her pinny and slippers. Lynn Margulis welcomes me and shows me into the study for a pre-breakfast interview for the radio programme I am making about her. This is a long, long way from the Chicago of her birth in 1938.

Lynn tells me the story of her childhood: Jackson Park, the rocks beyond the freeway by the lake, a visit to an island in the Mississippi where she felt at peace. Her parents liked to party and as the eldest child she learned detachment was necessary to get some thinking space. School, she told me, 'was a waste of time' and her adventurous intelligence got her into Chicago University at fourteen where she learned her intellectual attitudes and married soon-to-be famous cosmologist Carl Sagan at nineteen. 'I learned we chickens could do science,' she says. While she takes a year out from running her geosciences department at the University of Massachusetts, the Eastman House in Oxford goes with the job of visiting professor at Balliol College. Its study glows with polished wood and privilege, a hive of books spills from shelves and a precariously perched radio plays Schubert. These are the trappings of eminence and it has taken Lynn a long career to receive such establishment recognition and yet she is still a rebel. She occupies this place as a wonderfully exotic hybrid of don, defier and domestic.

Since the 1960s, Lynn has developed a theory of evolution called *symbiogenesis*. The orthodoxy in evolutionary science maintains the engine of evolutionary change is competition between organisms within a species and between species. Inspired by Russian scientists, ignored in the West during the Cold War, claiming cooperation was as important as competition, Lynn studied the development of cells and the role of symbiosis – the interaction between different organisms for mutual benefit. She developed the idea that in the early evolution of life, single-cell creatures without complex internal structures merged to form symbiotic relationships, which led to the formation of eukaryotic cells 3.5 billion years ago. Structures such as mitochondria in animals and plastids in plants, essential for creating energy, were once free-living bacteria or algae that became incorporated through ingestion or absorption by other cells to create the symbiotic life forms from which all multicellular organisms are descended. Rejected at first, this theory took over a decade to receive mainstream recognition. In the meantime, Lynn was working on something the establishment found even harder to swallow. She asserted that the whip or oar-like flagella and cilia organelles that single-cell organisms use to wriggle and swim with, the internal movements within cells and even cell division, also came from free-living creatures called spirochetes which became incorporated into symbiotic relationships with other cells and now allow them to move. This is still not accepted by mainstream science. There is an emotional side to the evolution of the cells we are made of and scientists are not immune to prejudice. When I asked Lynn why she received such hostility to the spirochete idea she just said, 'Maybe it's because they don't like the idea of their sperm tails coming from syphilis bacteria, I don't know.'

There's an attitude of both defiance and vulnerability in the way her bicycle leans in the hallway. The bike is one of a trinity of things beginning with B necessary for Lynn Margulis to feel at home: the other two are beauty and biophilia. Beauty could be this bright spring morning where pink flowers of Judas trees blossom under the honey-coloured stone of Oxford's dreaming spires. Biophilia is the love of wild Nature – a concept popularised by the biologist E.O. Wilson, who described Lynn as 'one of the most successful synthetic thinkers in modern biology'. And the bicycle is needed to propel the successful synthetic thinker through the beautiful streets of Oxford to meetings with other biophiliacs. Peddling science and a love of Nature is a story that goes way back for Lynn but it has brought her into conflict with some very powerful people. Neo-Darwinism – evolution as a synthesis determined by Darwin's theory of natural selection with Mendel's theory of inherited characteristics through the transfer of genes – has proved to be a powerful opposition to her work.

The high priest, to use Lynn's term, of neo-Darwinism is Richard Dawkins.

The evening before my breakfast appointment at Eastman House, Dawkins and Margulis shared the stage at Balliol College in a joint lecture entitled 'A Homage to Darwin'. The last time this happened there was a huge row. Lynn invited me to tag along to the pre-lecture dinner, a curious and rather surreal display of academic largess with polite conversation in a medieval dining hall at the centre of which Lynn drank beer from a pewter tankard with impish glee. The lecture was electric. The argument between two giants of evolutionary theory was fascinating and on home turf Dawkins wanted to appear as the voice of reason, patronising the eccentric Margulis as if he found her slightly deluded. For her part, Lynn was generous, inspiring and tough and it was hard to see why her ideas, backed up by evidence, provoked such antipathy from sections of the audience.

Some of this is to do with language. She says she sometimes feels like the only person speaking Polish in the room – everyone has to ignore you because they don't understand. Language again becomes important. Darwin's *On the Origin of Species* is loaded with phrases such as competition, struggle, survival, fitness, with little or no mention of cooperation or mutuality – qualities in Nature at the foundation of symbiogenesis she finds at least as important to evolution as competition. Lynn is wary of the unscientific use of terms such as 'competition' and 'cooperation': 'these may apply to banks or basketball teams,' she says, 'but not to understanding life.' She is angry when evolution is talked about as if it's a conflict between capitalism and communism with rigidly anglophone views of Victorian paternalism, which she says it often is. What she wants to say is that the unit of life is the nucleated cell which co-evolved with bacteria. We cannot understand biology without recognising the community nature of all life, whether in loose communities of single cells or tight communities in the form of animals, plants and fungi. Evolution, Lynn says, is the ecology of communities over time. When I asked her to sum up why she really objected to the neo-Darwinist view she said simply, 'Dawkins belongs to a tradition which took the life out of biology and I'm interested in life.'

Of all the things expected of an Eastman professor in their year at Balliol, I doubt making breakfast is one of them. Treading beech tree stamens from the garden onto the Eastman carpet, I join an odd salon of invited scientists and film-makers at the table. As Professor Margulis drops cashew nuts into breakfast bowls, I can't help thinking this strange normality has been paid for by some shuddering eureka moments of discovery and years of struggle. Lynn Margulis is a revolutionary.

A short while after my radio programme about Lynn, *A Life With Microbes*, was transmitted, she invited my wife Nancy and me to her leaving do. This time, Eastman House was full of eminent academics, environmentalists, influential scientists, professors of microbiology, deep ecologists and James Lovelock's daughters, people who admired and were inspired by her. Lynn has completed her year at Balliol and is going back to Amherst, Massachusetts where, as she liked to say, she lived next door to the poet Emily Dickinson who died there in 1886.

Not long after that, following a swim in Puffer's Pond, her favourite swimming hole in Amherst where she had recently discovered a new species of aquatic microbe, Lynn Margulis had a stroke and died, aged seventy-three. It was a shock, not least to her family, friends and students who could not believe such a unique force of Nature could just stop. Many people believe she should have received a Nobel Prize for her work on the development of the cell and many were inspired by her ideas on symbiosis, evolution and the new biology behind the Gaia hypothesis. Even those irritated by her more controversial pronouncements knew there was so much more to come from Lynn and so much more that deserved recognition.

There's a photograph on the Internet of Lynn swimming in Puffer's Pond with a caption that claims she is studying bryozoans in the water – slimy, colony-forming masses of interconnected individual organisms called moss animals. This particular species *Pectinatella magnifica*, the magnificent bryozoan, seems a uniquely appropriate creature to associate with Lynn, as is the quote from neighbour Emily Dickinson in a book Lynn co-authored with her son Dorian Sagan: 'The Truth must dazzle gradually/ Or every man be blind.'

AFIPIA

I shield my eyes against sunlight on the wing as I look through the porthole, waiting on the tarmac at Birmingham International airport. My plane is crowded and about to heave itself into the place of leaving. Taxi down the runway, thrust backward into the tilt at speed; there's nothing final or particular about the direction and trajectory of take-off but I wait for the exhilarating newness of it. When it happens, and I feel the simultaneous rising above of the plane and the falling below of the ground, a moment of excitement sweeps between on a rush of vertigo. Take-off is a guilty pleasure. Slewing over roofs and roads, higher now than crows and gulls then higher still than the skylark's whistling dot, into what?

Looking down on white clouds under an unerring blue, there is a relentlessness as far as I can see, an endless hostile beauty. I belong to the last generation to remember smoking cigarettes and drinking free alcohol on transatlantic flights, a kind of freedom which became an entitlement. Even though there is an increasing amount of (smoke-free) air travel I now feel a pang of guilt at flying at all, responsible for unnecessary pollution in a plane that should not be here, so high, so cold, so close to the sun and away from land. I am flying to America to report on a story about how atmospheric pollution affects wildlife. The conscience of our age has found the aeroplane to be a convenient cell in which to inhabit contested airspace: the freedom of the skies and the tyranny of global warming have become twin wings. And yet . . .

The outworld is beautiful and strange but inside bliss turns to boredom. False reality, enlivened by a bit of turbulence, is too bright. The steward wants me to draw the window blind so others can watch a film or nap. What is outside is an inconvenience; the minor unpleasantness of sunlight interrupts the complete abstraction from the world, like being in a diagram. We rise higher, a reaching-towards, inside the mirror tube, bright fish, with only my window blind open and I hope they hate me.

Now a white fuzziness has lowered into cloud tops, grey-stained as if wet, shadowed into rolling hills, plains and glacier crevasses; looming voids appear in an impossible place of beauty and great danger. Below the clouds must be the Atlantic Ocean but there's no telling from up here. Dust motes blaze across my eyes, perhaps beings travelling with me. The whiteness begins to break up into plateaus like huge lichen plates interspersed with grey-blue depths. Spaces open between the floes, deep blue with cloud islands, archipelagos, swirling spits and floating cloudbanks suspended. Way down there, white flecks of waves break in the actual sea which shines, rippling with patterned lines pitching, drawing diagonally against the pitted mercury. Stepping-stones of cloud lead west. I give in, having worn the opprobrium well enough I think, and draw the blind.

Enclosed in this dazzling cell wall, I am in international airspace, protected from an environment in which I cannot survive and yet cannot survive without. Up here in the troposphere, I wing through the zone of atmosphere which extends to 10 miles above the tropics and 5 miles above the poles. The higher we climb, the colder it gets: about minus 50 degrees centigrade. I draw the blind on the place where weather is made, the place of flux and circulation and mix where convection currents and jet streams travel the Earth, a place of turbulence where clouds are born. Here is the stirring of Earth's oxygen, water vapour, carbon dioxide, nitrogen and other gases; protected from the sun's ultraviolet radiation by the stratosphere above, allowing molecules to stabilise and make life possible. But then, all is possible because of life.

In 1974, Lynn Margulis and James Lovelock published a paper, not in an established scientific journal but a counterculture periodical called the *Whole Earth Catalog*, about Earth's atmosphere as a circulatory system actively controlled by living organisms, largely bacteria. This was the original public explanation of the Gaia hypothesis. Since then, the idea that Earth operates as a self-regulating living being through interconnected and interdependent relationships between living things and their environment has become accepted. Back then, a description of our life-supporting atmosphere being the product of life-supporting jimmy-wrigglers was nothing short of revolutionary. From its first public appearance, the Gaia hypothesis has been both seriously scientific and radically countercultural. Yet, however wonderful, this is probably not what the passengers in this plane want to contemplate at a cruising altitude of 40,000 feet with the blinds drawn. We are a congregation stuffed full of microbes flying through the miracle of evolution and yet we connect to gadgets that allow us to ignore it and instead watch films of our own dramas, comedies, tragedies. Nietzsche was right: we are the mad animal, the laughing, weeping, unhappy animal. We wriggle in our cell up in the troposphere but even here we are not alone; there is a microbiome knocking at the windows.

Samples of air from the middle to upper troposphere have been recently discovered to contain a surprising number of bacteria and fungi species. At lower levels, the skies are full of aerial plankton: seeds, spores, eggs, invertebrate larvae and tiny spiders ballooning on their threads. Higher up where conditions would appear to be far more hostile to life, even though they're created by it, the microbiome consists of beings from sea spume, whipped up by tropical storms and hurricanes, plant pathogens from soil that can promote freezing of ice in leaf membranes causing damage and promoting infection; even *Streptococcus* from human faeces. Some microbes are able to metabolise oxalic acid and live in the troposphere for some time while others, like me, are suspended in limbo, just passing through on a high-altitude long-haul journey. Scientists are interested in the atmospheric transport of disease transmission and pathogens; they have recognised this microbiome as a dynamic and under-appreciated aspect of the upper troposphere with potentially important impacts on the hydrological cycle, clouds and climate. At these altitudes, microbes have the ability to form a nucleus of ice around them and together create clouds. By far the most abundant group of bacteria in the troposphere samples is *Afipia* species – not the ones blamed for infections from cat-scratch but rod-like creatures from the sea that can survive in clouds using available carbon compounds present in the atmosphere and which belong to groups of *Oxalobacter* and *Methylobacterium* collected from cloud water. I sneak open the window blind to look at living clouds: *Afipia* sounds like a place, a country, a state, something like *epiphany*.

From my porthole in the flimsy fuselage I peer miles below into snow and ice, tundra, frosted white with blue-black lakes rippling with reflected clouds. There a river, sinuous through a stippled forest, snow-topped trees and peat hags, valleys edged silver; a road cuts through the river elbow, bright as a vein of quartz. Clouds thin over the tundra scattering fragments of shining air across a frozen river-lake-forest land. From spruce to aspen, pale green. In this Ice Age film below, water flows through a frozen world, through layers of sky, cloud, snow, permafrost. The white lakes are glaciers, beyond them bare rock, dark silty estuaries, gravel banks, land swirls, a lake of mother o' pearl shimmering and with a serpentine river. A gravel bank tailing off into a river looks like a massive *Paramecium* – the 'slipper animal' of biology textbooks so-called because of its shape which swims using a long whip-like tail or flagellum. At the edge, bogs give out into sea and a highway follows the coast, cutting across thawing tundra. No more ice: the sea is blue like swirling gas; there are long finger islands with farmed clearings and outwash silt bleeding into ultramarine. A sudden turbulence brings thick white cloud cover.

Gazing into the abyss, the abyss gazes back.

When I look at the clouds and land, rivers and sea, I know the laws of physics and chemistry are not operating in an inert environment; these huge planetary systems are driven by microbiological factors – life. Microbes are everywhere: around me in the upper atmosphere, below me in the soil, between ice crystals in glaciers, at the bottom of oceans and inside rocks. I am – me and my microbiome – in a plane full of aggregations of cells, travelling through the upper biosphere between ecosystems. And yet I do not feel it like that. To me, this experience does not feel like being in a scientific diagram divided into neatly labelled spheres, zones, strata, circulatory systems, ecosystems.

As a visual interpretation of Nature through the ecological relationships between things, I prefer paintings by Jackson Pollock; my favourite is *Autumn Rhythm*. This flight to America is the first time I've been back for many years. When I lived in New York State and worked at Quaker Hill botanical garden developing a collection of plant communities of eastern North American natives, I had opportunities to travel. After a trip to the Appalachians, studying the autumn colour of trees in woods, gardens and nursery specimens, I went with my family to the Museum of Modern Art in Manhattan. I wanted to see the big Pollock canvases and when I found *Autumn Rhythm No. 30*, the effect was so powerful, so full of my own experience of autumn woods and so numinous, I fell over. This may have been the result of what is called an autonomous sensory meridian response or not looking where I was going and tripping over a bench. But Pollock may have had no intention that his painting should represent Nature. Hans Hofmann, the painter and teacher with a huge influence on abstract expressionism, criticised Jackson Pollock in 1942 for working too little after Nature. Pollock famously replied, 'I am Nature.' This was not glib bravado. Pollock's friends maintained he had a deep empathy, sensibility and intensity in his approach to the non-human world. His earlier work was full of human-animal imagery, totemism, the merging of opposites and influences from prehistoric and so-called primitive art as well as the pantheism of the Indian spiritual writer and teacher Krishnamurti. Pollock was rejecting the civilisation that had produced the Second World War; he was the painter as shaman, a link between the wildness of Nature and a collective unconscious.

Perhaps something of this sensory response to Pollock's paintings and the way they take on a life of their own spills over into my attraction to the Gaia hypothesis. The author William Golding came up with the name Gaia. Lovelock's hypothesis was that life itself regulates our planetary systems so that the Earth acts as if it were a single organism. Gaia was an alternative spelling of the Greek Earth goddess Gea and used in Earth sciences such as geology, geophysics and geography. Paradoxically, Gaia was a new yet ancient way of thinking about Earth and life and everything and even though I am sceptical of the Earth as a single organism idea, which even Lynn Margulis thought didn't work, I appreciate the strength of a metaphor that may get people to care about the planet. However, that too is loaded with evangelism, the persuasion of the ignorant, the exploitative and profligate onto the path of environmental righteousness. I am also sceptical of the quasi-religious aspects of Gaia: the re-feminisation of Mother Earth strikes me as patronising anthropomorphism and previous religious beliefs and humanisms about creation and the human place on Earth are replaced with an alternative and equally zealous faith and creed. Earth is plagued by big ideas: they shape the minds that surround me; hoist this thing we travel in through the skies; pave the highway down below to the deep north with good intentions. Once back on land, to see smoke rising behind the towers of Philadelphia, I will double back to investigate a Gaian story about atmosphere, microbes and one of the north's most enigmatic birds.

MAHNG

I'm being zipped inside a tent with a gap left at the top of the flap to peer out from. I can just about see between branches of black spruce into the grey windy space of Brassua Lake and the sky above the Great North Woods of Maine. I love this glimpse of a tree-water-hills-sky world, a pre-agricultural or perhaps post-agricultural vision of my own countryside, like the feeling I got as a child from backwoods pictures and old black and white films such as George Seitz's 1936 adaptation of James Fenimore Cooper's novel *The Last of the Mohicans*. Hiding in the brush on this wooded island, the size of an average back garden, are five men and a bloodhound and sitting next to me in the tent hide is David Evers. Dave is an ornithologist who has spent his life studying the bird the Native American Iroquois call Mahng, Americans call loons and the British call great northern divers. The song of Mahng is evocative of northern lakes – North America, Britain, Scandinavia and northern Russia – and as enigmatic as a wolf's howl. A recording of a loon's call plays at intervals through a megaphone across the 12-mile stretch of still water on Brassua Lake. Although rather tinny and distorted, the sound is a haunting wail that slides from heartbreak to defiance.

I am unaware at first that a real loon has heard the call; to him it's a threat, a challenge to his territory. He comes steaming across the lake at ramming speed, his eyes burning. The poet of the Maine woods Henry Wadsworth Longfellow (1807–1882) named the hero in his poem *The Song of Hiawatha*, *Mahng-go-tay'see*. In the native language, this meant loon-hearted brave, a way of capturing the bird's fearless reputation in the name of a warrior. As the loon is lured to the source of his challenger's call he is caught in a net trap, a new twist on an old hunting trick. Dave Evers and his team of field biologists quickly capture the bird; they allow me to hold it while they take measurements and samples of feather and blood. I am shown how to keep it secure so it doesn't injure itself or me. The loon is an astonishing creature: a goose-sized duck with an iridescent green head, burning red eyes and a dagger beak. His legs and powerful webbed feet are set back on his body to propel him underwater hunting fish; they are almost useless on land. His plumage is patterned black and white like a condensed version of the rock and ice landscape I saw from the plane. The poet Gerard Manley Hopkins says of such pied beauty that it is 'All things counter, original, spare, strange . . .'.

The reason for subjecting this courageous and charismatic bird to such indignity is mercury. Dave has been studying the effects of mercury pollution on loons for many years and his findings are worrying. Loons contain so much mercury that it affects their young and 40 per cent of fledgling loons are being lost to a poison we are responsible for. Looking at this remote lake in the Great North Woods it seems unlikely there should be so much mercury pollution, which I had assumed came from industrial waste. Dave explains that other researchers around the world have found increasing mercury loads in remote environments and much of it comes from coal-fired power stations. I think of the cooling towers and high chimney of Buildwas power station I see from Wenlock Edge and imagine what the years of burning coal there have done to the populations of loons – great northern divers – in Britain, Europe, even here; how switching my lights on is killing them off. Atmospheric pollution is carried through the troposphere thousands of miles from its source. When it lands, the mercury is inert but is acted upon by microbes which create toxins from it. In freshwater ecosystems such as Brassua Lake, these mercury toxins travel through the food chain into fish which are hunted by loons. Here is just one story of Gaia, the biological power of microbes and a darker ecology in which the human drive to improve life for ourselves is destroying wild lives we have no real conception of. Can people turning their lights on, boiling their kettles and charging their phones exert any more responsibility for the ecological consequences of their actions than the microbes making mercury available to the food chain? That question changes when I ask what responsibility *I* have.

In *The Revenge of Gaia* (2006), James Lovelock breaks the news that Gaia is suffering from a 'morbid fever'. The human 'plague' responsible for global heating from greenhouse gases, the loss of Arctic ice, the changing structure of oceans and destruction of tropical forests is afflicting an ageing, far less resilient, living planet. Like many environmental writers and journalists, I made the trip to James Lovelock's house in the Devon countryside. I went for a walk with him: white-haired and less resilient himself, he was unassumingly sage-like, charming, generous with his time and ideas; we talked and walked around his garden, along an abandoned railway line under trees, across a field and back. In forty years of the hypothesis, Gaia has undergone a metamorphosis. From an innocent self-consciousness, 'through our eyes she has for the first time seen her very fair face and in our minds become aware of herself', Gaia has become, 'an old lady who has to share her house with a growing and destructive group of teenagers, Gaia grows angry, and if they do not mend their ways she will evict them.' In my view, Gaia has responded to ecophobia and become the threat of retribution.

That threat looks back at me through the scarlet eye of the loon. As waves slap against the island there's a cold wind skidding down Brassua Lake bringing rain. This loon has been out of the water for long enough and Dave is itching to get it back into the wild again. It has sacrificed blood, feathers and more importantly its freedom and made an important contribution to the understanding of the species in its ecosystem. Dave Evers and his crew are going about their work as quickly and efficiently as possible to reduce any distress. Everyone here, including the bloodhound – who watches protectively – has the greatest respect for the bird, not just because of its courage and charisma but also because of what it can reveal about the world it inhabits. They are working with other scientists, companies and government departments around the world to provide evidence of pollution loads on ecosystems and stimulate the political will to deal with it. They are pragmatic optimists. Dave knows the loon holds the key to understanding and protecting these wild places. The bird can be released and as if to show his appreciation Mahng craps all over me. I consider it a privilege. *Mahng-go-tay'see* takes off across Brassua Lake, his wings slapping the surface until he is far enough away. Then he pauses, composes himself and throws an eerily defiant wail out across the water and the great woods into the sky.

IO.
PLOT

A defined piece of ground; to mark out on a map or chart; the interrelationships between events in a play or novel; a conspiracy or secret plan.

GREAT SPOTTED WOODPECKER

Distracted, I tap the table with my pencil like Morse code and then more rapidly like a woodpecker drumming on a tree until this thought pops out: *gardening is the performance of the movement of Nature into culture.* That's what occurs to me in a transport caff somewhere in north Shropshire one fine autumn morning. I'm sitting at the back of an empty cafe and on the table is a mug of tea and a book on the New Biology. I'm reading about how the biology of the nineteenth and twentieth centuries presented the concept of the Tree of Life as a graph showing the connections between species in an order which reflects their common ancestry. This human-imposed hierarchy is now complicated by a new understanding of branching histories: the ways genes are shuffled about between species and symbiogenesis – the theory of evolution in which new cell organelles, new bodies, new organs and new species arise from symbiosis – independent organisms joining together and relying on cooperation as much as competition. Big windows let in a sugary light, yellow as birch leaves, flickering with passing trade. I have driven to somewhere unfamiliar in the hope it helps me think about some of these ideas that I want to use in my writing. What happens is that these ideas begin to permeate my own tree-of-life history.

It turns out this area should feel more familiar than it does. Little Johnny Evans, my great-grandfather, had a dog-and-stick farm – so-called because that's the most basic equipment for herding cattle – near here. His eldest son, John, was killed under the wheels of a cart. His other two sons, Arthur and Eric, my grandfather, didn't want to be tenant farmers but stayed fairly local and when they died we lost the direct connection with this land of meres, mosses and sandstone ridges which stick out of the plain like stumbling blocks. Whenever I pass through this part of the county I feel a strange belonging; nostalgia for a place and time I have never experienced. Perhaps some unconscious feeling of uprootedness draws me here as if the tragedy of my great-uncle's death broke the line in a story that needs mending. Perhaps my years of working as a gardener in plots of ground which don't belong to me go some way to grafting myself into that old peasant myth of men and land. Many of us are only a couple of generations away from that story. Anyway, this roadside greasy spoon in ancestral territory turns out to be the place where I begin to understand what twenty years as a gardener has been all about: *gardening is the performance of the movement of Nature into culture.*

I imagine the symbiosis, the merging of abstract ideas as if they were independent organisms: Nature – because it contains us – is not entirely natural. Culture – because it is infiltrated by wild Nature – is not entirely cultural. It is an error to believe the Nature we think of as wholly natural – in that it's not been tampered with by people – becomes something completely different when it's in gardens we think of as wholly cultural – in that they are designed, built and managed by people. But the act of gardening, the performance of cultivation, is the movement of wild Nature into culture: the drama of civilisation. I think of gardens in which I have worked in England, Wales and America: Canley Garden Cemetery – garden maintenance and grave filler-in, Wellington Parks Department – mobile maintenance gangs and nursery worker, Percy Thrower's Garden Centre – woody plant propagator, Powis Castle – craftsman gardener, Chirk Castle – gardener in charge, Quaker Hill – horticultural director of native plant botanical garden, David Austin Roses – plant centre designer and manager. I think of those I have visited: municipal parks, churchyards, burial grounds, gardens of remembrance, allotments, botanical gardens, wild gardens, permaculture gardens, forest gardens, tropical gardens, desert oases, urban oases, stately home gardens, rooftop gardens, suburban gardens, city gardens, cottage gardens, temple gardens, courtyard gardens, show gardens, derelict gardens. Although these are very different places worked in different ways for different reasons, there are powerful similarities between them. Gardens tell a story about the relationship between the wild and civilisation which began a very long time ago. Nomadic hunter-gatherers may have found plants of great value in forest clearings, pools or hilltops, which they protected from encroaching undergrowth, fenced against browsers with an enclosure of sticks, marked for future foragers. These unplanned, unplanted places became gardens visited seasonally before the Neolithic revolution when wild animals were domesticated and wild plants cultivated.

The garden historian Miles Hadfield in *A History of British Gardening*, begins with the Garden of Eden, 'Such was the place in which the first of all gardeners, who, with ditchers and gravediggers alone can claim to be an ancient gentleman, was set.' For me the history of the garden, from ancient Egyptians through to the Romans who brought it to Britain, began with an old tin bathtub. I was very young, with my net made out of nylon stockings on a long stick, teetering on the dark edges of old reservoirs and woodland pools to collect long green fingers of Canadian pondweed and flag-iris tubers from stinky black ooze. I picked beautifully whorled pond snails which were supposed to give sheep liver fluke and caddis fly larvae which looked like tiny monsters hiding in sleeping bags camouflaged with bits of twig and grit. More by luck than judgement, I netted jerky water boatmen, dragon-crested newts and scarlet-bellied, thorny sticklebacks in jam jars for my bathtub pond sunk in the back garden. This was a place of wonders and immediately linked wildlife to gardening in a way that has stuck with me throughout my life. Just Add Water, may have been a motto shared between the irrigation genius of the hanging gardeners of Babylon, the ecology of modern conservationists and my own boyhood.

In my gardening career I felt a comradeship with ditchers and gravediggers in common service to our patch, place or plot. As well as inclinations towards stubbornness, we shared a backache from the jolt, jar or yield of the land carried up an ash handle from the sharp end of a spade. However, I knew the green arts, the magic of gardening, was of a very different order. Digging ditches and graves, even though mostly done with machines now, is still a raw, rude and solitary performance, hidden acts deliberately avoiding acclaim or imitation. I remember gravediggers in the Coventry cemetery where I worked covering the soil they dug with clean green hessian to hide the savage earth from mourners, and hide themselves in a shed as a mark of respect. There are not many television programmes about ditching and gravedigging. Gardening is a public performance: to dig and delve, snip and saw, mulch and mow are part of a repertoire of rituals through which cultivation creates something of great value. From the eighteenth century, gardening became Britain's most important contribution to European culture. In castle or cottage, whatever size the plot, the garden aesthetic was both socially imitative and egalitarian, maintained by privileged knowledge and simple rituals practised to exert power over Nature. Historian Keith Thomas in *Man and the Natural World* (1984), said, 'The preoccupation with gardening . . . even helps to explain the relative lack of radical and political impulses among the British proletariat.' Ceremonial practices in the cult of lawns and roses – are they why we never had a revolution?

Instinctively, I feel the subversive presence of the wild in such rituals: there is no rose without greenfly, lawn without molehill, cabbage without caterpillar. Our feelings for gardening take their cues from the community of life we are part of. The passion for mowing and pruning simulates the parkland or savannah landscapes formed by the grazing and browsing of big herbivores. The love of flowers which D.H. Lawrence thought was 'merely this reaching out of possession and egoism . . .' is what drives the bee and butterfly aesthetic. The desire to sow seed mimics the work of ants and thrushes. The legacy of great oaks for the future replicates the acorn-stashing of jays. These creative impulses find their way into gardening from Nature. Gardening makes places in which we feel safe, places the landscape theorist Jay Appleton has described as designed for prospect – to see what's coming – and refuge – to conceal ourselves from it. I argue, what we want a prospect of and a safe refuge from is wild Nature itself. Despite the best efforts of loyal gardeners, the war against wild Nature was not only lost the day Eden was made, it was a necessary deception in the making of civilisation. A phoney war against wilderness created an adversarial approach to Nature. People who inhabited wilderness were primitives; people who colonised wilderness to cultivate it were heroes. The control of Nature is necessary to keep us safe and preserve civilised values. Even in modern times, an abhorrence of an unkempt garden, the moral dereliction of an overgrown plot, teaches ecophobia: a fear of Nature getting out of hand. These anxieties are the glue that bonds cultivation to civilisation.

One New Year's Day I walked into the Wilderness to inspect the damage from the previous night's storm. It was not uncommon for large estates to have a Wilderness or woodland garden with paths and vistas spiced up with specimens from the colonies. Since the seventeenth century, trees and shrubs collected from previously remote parts of the world opened up by exploration, colonisation and trade, had been planted among native trees to create a wooded Elysium and a 'wild' form of garden as an antidote to intensely formal styles. Pines and redwoods from North America, monkey puzzles from Chile, rhododendrons from the Himalayas, maples and magnolias from Japan, handkerchief trees from China, southern beech from New Zealand. These plants arrived bringing with them an exoticism and drama at a time when British woodland was being embraced by Romantic art. I had some responsibility for the Wilderness Garden and although its name was an oxymoron, I was very fond of its old oaks, tall conifers, rhododendron tangles, its woodland shadows hiding their botanical and archaeological treasures. It was a place apart, quite unlike the towering yew hedges, terraces of luxuriant herbaceous borders and sweeping lawns of the rest of Powis Castle gardens near Welshpool in mid-Wales. Powis is a medieval fortress which became a grand, red-stone mansion. Centuries of gardening styles overlap here but much of the formal gardens, terraces and hedges are still extant. The gardens are surrounded by a deerpark, forests, farms and the sweeping green county of Montgomeryshire which became subsumed within the county named after the old Welsh principality of Powys.

The Wilderness was strange, theatrical, and it absorbed me. My work in it was a performance which maintained its mysterious, shadowy life. And so it was a shock to see one of its most spectacular trees so badly damaged. A fall of wet snow and gale-force winds had been too much for the high flat branches of a cedar of Lebanon. Half the tree lay on the ground, dark green-needled boughs so huge when laid out in the snow, jagged wounds where they had been ripped from the trunk above. The cedar was over two hundred years old and although magnificent in its spread and girth, it was approaching the end of its natural life in this part of the world, even though it was less than half the age of native oaks in the Wilderness. New Year's Eve was ominous: traumatic for the tree and both unsettling and exciting for the gardeners whose tranquillity and sense of continuity had been overwhelmed by Nature's violence. It represented an opening to a very different future. We found ourselves in a drama: a tragedy that turned to comedy. Our first response was to try to restore the cedar: patch the tree up, tidy the wounds so they would not rot and remove the fallen branches. Three of us erected a 60-foot ladder, strung some old washing line to hold on to and scrambled into the place where the uppermost branches had broken off with a chainsaw hired for the first time that morning. I didn't even know how to start it. What the hell were we doing?

The scent of resin and timber was overwhelming: sweet, spicy, warm, intoxicating; this was the fragrance from faraway Arz el-Rob, the Cedars of God, a sacred forest on Mount Lebanon. Gilgamesh, the legendary Mesopotamian king (between 2800 and 2500 BC), smelled this when he built his city from cedarwood, as did Phoenician shipwrights their fleets and Ottomans their railways. Plundered for centuries, the Cedars of God were once protected by a wall donated by Queen Victoria. This great tree, now so broken, must have been seen by Victoria when she was a child on a visit to Powis Castle in 1832; I like to think it inspired her. Without a trace of irony, Mount Lebanon may have been our first overseas nature reserve and how appropriately for the British to enclose such a wild, sacred place with a garden wall. I wondered why a forest giant adapted to mountain snows had become so brittle here and I felt a responsibility to help. Dangling at the top of the broken cedar, I realised I needed help too; at least, I needed training in arboriculture.

From up there I could see from the Wilderness at Powis Castle across the Severn valley to another collection of exotic trees on the Leighton estate. The arboretum there was established by C.J. Leyland in the nineteenth century and although it slipped into obscurity, Leyland left a historical footnote metaphorically nailed to a tree which was to have a huge impact on the British landscape and beyond. A hybrid cypress was discovered at Leighton in 1888. Its parents had been introduced into Britain some years earlier from the west coast of North America, but they would never have met in the wild. The Nootka cypress, *Chamaecyparis nootkatensis*, came from the strip of Pacific temperate rainforest which extends from Alaska to northern Oregon. This is a forest tree that grows to 200 feet tall with beautiful pendulous foliage. The Monterey cypress, *Cupressus macrocarpa*, is from the low sea cliffs of Cypress Point and Point Lobos near Monterey, California and although not nearly as tall as the Nootka cypress is of huge girth and width. These two trees originated over 1,000 miles apart and would never have hybridised naturally until something weird happened in Wales.

Leyland discovered some seedlings of his Nootka cypress had hybridised naturally with a nearby Monterey cypress and grew them on. In 1911, his nephew Captain Naylor attempted the cross in reverse and got seedlings of the

Monterey crossed with the Nootka. Kew Gardens acquired these hybrids in 1925 and nurseries began to get interested. The hybrids were of great botanical importance because they were naturally bigenic, of parents from two separate genera, like crossing cats with dogs, a very rare occurrence in Nature. They combined the grace of the Nootka with the salt-tolerance and bulk of the Monterey. They would grow in any soil, stand up to fierce winds, they were free of pests and disease, bone hardy and grew like rockets. However, it was not until the 1960s, with advances in propagation techniques, container growing and the rise of the garden centre, that the commercial potential of the hybrid trees called Leyland cypress became realised. Marketed as the ultimate in fast-growing hedges, screens and windbreaks, demand for Leyland cypress, x*Cupressocyparis leylandii*, outstripped supply. From its obscure origins, it is estimated there are 55 million *leylandii* in Britain – one in five British trees is now a *leylandii*. One in every two trees planted is a *leylandii* and over 300,000 of them are sold every year.

The status of the Leyland cypress changed from godsend to monster in twenty years – about as long as it takes this tree, or a hedge of them, to reach 40 feet tall. Because of an estimated 100,000 ugly disputes between neighbours either side of a *leylandii* hedge, legislation has been introduced to empower local authorities to intervene. This contested tree has certainly supported the arboriculture industry. The problem really stems from the British obsession with privacy, enclosure and instant gratification that led to the planting of trees which intend to become a temperate rainforest of the future. The original trees at Leighton have been felled or blown down; Kew lost its specimens in the 1990 gales; Bedgebury arboretum has *leylandii* planted in 1933 that are now 130 feet tall. No one knows how big they will grow because there are no fully grown *leylandii* yet. Much maligned in some quarters as an environmental disaster, they were described by British tree expert Alan Mitchell as 'a 1960s towerblock for birds, it provides habitat for 20–30 species of birds, notably siskins, goldcrests and firecrests'. Overgrown *leylandii* hedges in a suburb of Shrewsbury harboured a murmuration of starlings over a million strong. The experience at dusk of watching starlings dance like smoke through the sky then disappear into these dark trees was astonishing and beautiful. Local residents, frightened by the swarm, complained about their cars being crapped on and wanted the *leylandii* felled to remove the starlings.

Leyland's cypress is a story of our times. It carries a narrative that speaks of our relationship with Nature and each other through an obsession with enclosure and anxieties about control. Although its parent species were introduced from the other side of the world and the plant was in part the result of the Frankenstein laboratory of horticulture, it occurred as a natural hybrid.

This is also the case for a range of novel organisms that are changing forests around the world and have arrived in Britain through the horticulture industry: the *Phytophthoras*. Their name means plant-destroyer and their fearful reputation goes back to the blight which caused the Irish potato famine from 1845 to 1860. Sometimes called water moulds or fungi, they are in fact *Oomycota*, kinds of protists that include some brown algae and slime moulds. Unlike fungi the *Oomycota* have diploid chromosomes, cell walls of cellulose, and can reproduce by cell division, store food as starch and produce spores that swim like animals through water. However, *Phytophthoras* spread through the host plants like a fungus and can cause root rot, stem rot, leaf blight and bleeding cankers. Sudden oak death, *P. ramorum*, is such a virulent pathogen of oaks and other trees in America that it is decimating forests. It affected its first British tree in 2003. The global horticulture trade and the movement of plants from around the world has brought geographically distinct species of *Phytophthora* together which would otherwise have no possibility of meeting in the wild.

Plants which have never encountered these pathogens have no immunity to them and this can be devastating. New *Phytophthora* hybrids are emerging and a possible hybrid of *P. ramorum* was discovered in Cornwall in 2003 called *P. kernoviae*, affecting beech, rhododendron and oak species. Another hybrid, *P. alni*, came from European tree nurseries to Britain in 1993 and is travelling through British river systems killing alder trees. A *Phytophthora* recognised in the United States since the 1930s began affecting British horse chestnut trees in the 1970s. This was not common here until about 2004 when incidence of bleeding cankers on the trunks and main branches and leaf blight on the trees began to increase massively. This turns out to be caused by the bacteria *Pseudomonas syringae pv aesculi*. It is a sub-species of *Psuedomonas syringae* – one of the commonest organisms from the sample of microbes taken from 30,000 feet up in the troposphere – and it is found in atmospheric aerosols, clouds and hailstones; and because it can form ice around itself it is responsible for frost damage in many plants. Another new and dramatic tree pathogen is the fungus *Hymenoscyphus pseudoalbidus* which causes ash dieback. This virulent form is virtually the same as *Hymenoscyphus albidus*, a fungus of ash leaves which has been around for ages and does not have a lethal effect. It is also the same as a Chinese fungus that lives harmlessly on a Chinese species of ash. These previously benign fungi seem to have combined to form one of the most virulent tree pathogens of modern times. Ash dieback was thought to have emerged from European tree nurseries and spread by transporting infected trees but now it is understood that the fungal spores can travel in winds from the continent as well.

These protists, fungi and bacteria, like Lawson's cypress, are the unintentional consequences of cultivation, globalisation and the industrialisation of gardening. The story of *ergasiophygophytes*, the plants that jump the garden wall to colonise the countryside, is an old one. Although this has become a disaster in many parts of the world, and I'm reminded of the shocking destruction wrought by introduced garden plants on the Juan Fernández Islands, the major threat to British plants comes from other British plants – bramble, bracken and ivy. Changes in land use, management and climate have released some native species to overwhelm others. Conservation, as a form of cultivation evolved from gardening, is the performance of protecting the Nature we like – the aesthetic – from the Nature we don't like. However, these escapes, hybridisations and rapid adaptations are a natural evolutionary process that is undoing the forests of the past and creating forests of the future. As Lynn Margulis might say, 'this is community dynamics over time'.

As a gardener and nature conservationist, I am fascinated by the way our attitudes to wild and cultivated plants shape the world we live in. Like many, I am deeply concerned that the threat to wild plants from farming, industry and development, which destroys their places, pollutes their air, water and soil and changes the climate, is a threat to life on Earth. And yet, how might they be 'saved'? Conservation is a form of cultivation which manages plants based on how they matter to people. Advocacy for wildness, a setting free of the ecological processes that shape plant communities, also depends on ways in which they matter to us. I think we need an ethical common ground that includes both wild plants and cultivated ones. Flower or weed, friend or foe, edible or poisonous, these preferences or prejudices stem from conflicts between cultivation and wildness. Plants such as wheat, soya and opium poppy have changed human society. While plants such as rose, lotus and chrysanthemum have had a significant meaning for culture. Oak trees are both cultivated and wild and as well as traditionally providing timber, panage for pigs, shade, habitat for hundreds of kinds of wildlife, boundary markings and symbols of nationhood, they are venerated in a kind of vernacular worship; oaks are cherished as beautiful and significant in their own right.

Plants naturally form communities. Sometimes these have been assembled directly by people, as in gardens.

Sometimes plant communities are formed indirectly as a consequence of land use, as in woods and heaths; or not at all influenced by people, as in mountain cliffs and salt marsh. Even those plants that have no obvious human benefit are valued for their beauty or as the distinctive language of a place. These plant communities have to include the symbiosis of soil microbes and fungi on which they depend, as well as pollinating insects and grazing animals that influence their composition. If we then include ourselves in these communities of place, we are reacting against the placelessness that our modern Western industrialised culture has achieved in distancing itself from Nature. However we try to control the Nature we bring into culture, however sophisticated we believe our management of natural processes to be, the more fearful we will become of Nature's response. New communities of place are forming that not only include ourselves but weeds and pathogens we have struggled against. Inadvertently, by moving Nature into culture, gardening has created a space between these two states where a very different kind of wilderness is emerging.

My view of the Wilderness from 70 feet up the storm-damaged cedar of Lebanon changes. Conifers taller than the surrounding deciduous canopy, which rise like spires above rooftops, will be removed for aesthetic reasons. Thickets of rhododendron will be grubbed up to prevent harbouring *Phytophthora* pathogens. Dead limbs will be amputated to improve the health of trees. Hollow trunks and those posing a danger to visitors will be lopped or felled. This cedar, its architecture unbalanced, will continue to break up in storms and so it will be cut down, its stump ground out of the earth and within a few years will be forgotten, as if it never existed. All this begins with my pull-start and the chainsaw screaming into life, the voice of a new era. The air is full of light, the sharp edge of a breeze and the music of destruction. Like an electric guitar labouring through a couple of chords, the chainsaw goes about its relentless business. I remember how that feels: the sense of power as the chain bites through timber; the smell of chain-oil, fuel and flying sawdust; the thrill of working high in the trees where senses are sharpened by danger. And yet the sound of chainsaws represents something dark. What has taken years, sometimes centuries to grow can be reduced to a pile of logs and dust in a matter of minutes. Chainsaws create a soundtrack for human chauvinism in ways that the sound of axes does not. With an axe, each blow rings down the centuries, linking iron with stone and a kind of labour which is thousands of years old and fits with the landscape. It's the scale and speed of destruction which chainsaws enable that gives them such power. Because of this power, the technology has taken over. In woods and forests around the world the chainsaws rev, whine and scream through their savage repertoire, unleashing arboricide.

At the very opposite end of this spectrum, but not far away, a woodpecker drums on a branch. Piebald and red, the bird walks along high branches, stopping to throw its high piping call into clear air, then hammers on the branch to make a drumming which carries far into the treetops. Searching for insects along a dead bough which rises skyward, the woodpecker becomes an emblem which stands against the chainsaw and a reason for leaving trees alone. But the music of destruction is loud and the world is deaf.

Gardeners had been working in the Wilderness for 300 years before me. They worked for aristocrats and their head gardeners in a feudal enclave which changed little over the years. Even though Powis Castle and its famous gardens had been taken over by the National Trust in 1952, it was reluctant to change the gardens' old ways and so the structures of management and the general pace and rhythm of work remained very similar. However, under the leadership of head gardener Jimmy Hancock, the culture of the gardens became much more benign, creative and progressive. In the 1970s, we were a community, a kind of nature reserve for eccentrics. Apart from revitalising the plantings, particularly the hanging terraces of herbaceous wonders and a formalising of the gardening profession, perhaps the most significant change in those years was the shift from private indulgence to public good. Historic gardens, particularly those owned by the National Trust such as Powis Castle, were not going to become collective landscapes in the way Victorian municipal parks had evolved but they were very influenced by communities of interest beyond the one which lived and worked there. Public, charitable and voluntary bodies concerned with conservation, architecture, landscape and environment saw their prime duty as stewards, holding the land in trust for future generations, preserving 'our' heritage so that it might become theirs. This heritage was an appropriation of Nature in a much wider sense and included not only places of historical and aesthetic interest but also the environments of the biosphere and atmosphere. Heritage, both natural and cultural, was also linked to well-being and stewardship of these resources was seen as a public good which underpinned every aspect of life. Gardening moved Nature into culture in the form of heritage. The public appetite for this grew insatiably and the number of visitors to Powis, as elsewhere, rocketed.

Garden visiting, a very old tradition, became increasingly popular with the rise of heritage tourism, the horticultural press and television programmes. I worked for the first of the television gardeners, Percy Thrower, before Powis Castle and glimpsed the curious Wizard of Oz world behind the cameras and have been involved in a few TV programmes myself. Gardening, exploding as a popular art form, had been influenced by the Picturesque landscape movement since the eighteenth century. By bringing wild Nature and a pastoral vision of Arcadia together in paintings, art's civilising influence shaped the way landscapes were constructed and managed. This way of seeing Nature was so popular that it spanned the social divide to become the landscape of the English psyche; a ghost-ridden heritage of deception that continues into the twenty-first century. The seducing ethos of the Picturesque lay in its apparent naturalness; its intimacy and the diversity of the woodland scene as exemplified by the Wilderness garden was really at the root of the domestic garden. In 1877, the Canadian science writer, novelist and evolution supporter Grant Allen, in *Physiological Aesthetics*, suggested that human senses and perceptions had evolved from forest dwelling long before we moved out into savannah landscapes. All people had to do to reach back into their evolutionary origins was to lie in a garden looking upwards through foliage. The reverse is also true. I had a similar intuition from the top of the cedar of Lebanon on a New Year's Day long ago. In that wild place where the storm had ripped off branches, I was standing, absurdly, in the deep past. And from up there I could see into the future.

DORMOUSE

From out of the grey comes a flock, a grind of blackbirds, to the rowan tree. The berries have looked scarlet-ripe for months but birds don't seem to have been interested until now. Only over the last few days, when night and morning temperatures feel more like winter, have the berries begun to fall from the tree. Perhaps it's linked with the waxing moon but there have only been rowan berries on the ground for the last few days and now they are being eaten. The blackbirds perch on the twig ends next to berry clusters and pick them one by one, their beaks like needle-nosed pliers, holding each red berry for a moment before swallowing it whole.

I can't tell but my guess is these are migrant blackbirds that come here from the Netherlands, Germany and southern Scandinavia for the winter. There is something about their energy and presence that makes them subtly different from the locals. Perhaps some blackbirds from the Baltic island pine woods of Finnhamn are here. The British blackbirds, those that set up breeding territories locally and stay year round, have probably not moved far away. Males and females may remain in the general territory although not in the same place. There has been a lot of blackbird sound recently. Apart from the usual discipline-keeping clucking, which sounds like disappointment and complaint, there have been more spirited, aggressive *seees* and *chink-chink* calls which may be caused by friction between the stay-at-homes and the incomers. Maybe it's excitement and they have known each other for years. Together, they perceive – as we have heard on weather forecasts – that Arctic conditions are set to move in and they need to feed up on the rowan berries whose ripening has been triggered by the moon.

Other seasonal signature fruits ripen, too. Redder than remembrance poppies, riper than a bunch of tomatoes, poisonous as hell, the hedge is swagged in black bryony berries. After what feels like weeks of rain, the first day out of the murk is a spark blown on tinder. From the gate into the wood on the old holloway up Wenlock Edge from Homer, the day brightens from scattered embers of sunlight caught in distant places: the market tower, church spires and retail parks of Shrewsbury; the stumbling block hills of Haughmond, Grinshill and Hawkstone near my great-grandfather's farm; the far smokestack of the chipboard factory at Chirk across the Welsh border behind which we lived at the Pretty Gates and worked in Chirk Castle gardens; the high slopes of the Berwyns on the horizon; the Breidden Hills and the long ridge beyond where Powis Castle looks back . . . I become wistful, floaty. My eyes follow patches of sunlight over long fields, woods and hills – *hiraeth*. And yet, there it is, my homeland. Many years ago, living in Shrewsbury and cycling to work at Percy Thrower's Garden Centre, I would pause on Ditherington railway bridge to look west at the Shropshire Hills and the Welsh Marches and get the same feeling. Years after that I would gaze east from the Wilderness in Powis Castle gardens at the other side of the same hills and have the same feeling of *hiraeth*.

Gradually, with a sense of release from torpor, sunlight sets fire to winter. Along hedges where the bryony berries shine, the sunlight is snagged on spiders' webs. They float in the air and stroke against my skin as I walk through them. Thousands of spiders, spinning, weaving and casting gossamer, trap the light. All this silence is too much for the birds. After days of lockdown they are ready to burst with sound. It begins with the cough and growl of a raven above the brook. Rancorous wrens bolt from ivy holes to zigzag across lanes. Gangs of redwings go scrumping through trees. Buzzards ditch their plaintive appeals to sound fearsome firework screams. Soon the birds of hedge, field and wood are tearing about recklessly in this new light. In a cluster of bryony berries, a spider feels the twitch of silk through its long reach and suddenly, as only spiders can, throws itself into the present. In some strange way this movement is the fragment of a song, a bite, a flash – an inspired act of insurgence.

Fluted finger-length pillars rise ghostly pale to support roofs the size of handkerchiefs as if they were alien creatures breathing through hundreds of delicate gills and ill prepared for daylight and air. They come as a shock – the honey fungus mushrooms. The apple tree trunk has been leaning for years with old wounds indicating dead wood but it has always been a good-doer. This year saw a gradual sickening: fewer, smaller, jaundiced leaves; thin, brittle-looking stems; sparse little apples instead of great fat cookers thudding into the grass. Suddenly, as if out of nowhere, the base of the apple tree is sprouting honey-coloured mushrooms, *Armillaria mellea*. I suspected honey fungus was around in an old garden on land worked since medieval times and probably earlier. This beautiful fungus is a pathogen of living wood, white rot, and spreads by 'bootlaces': black sheathed rhizomorphs containing parallel bundles of hyphae like fibre-optic cables. These bootlaces can grow many metres through soil from where the fungus is devouring a rotting stump or root to parasitise a new host in living wood. Some years ago, scientists investigating *Armillaria* in a forest in Crystal Falls, Michigan, claimed the fungus was a single organism which covered 15 hectares, weighed 9,700 kilograms (heavy as a blue whale) and was 1,500 years old. I wonder if the bootlaces that have found the apple tree reach from an older forest in a time before Wenlock was a Saxon settlement around its Abbey. *Armillaria* is a gardener's curse and I have seen its work often: just when a tree is at its most mature and beautiful, it is taken as a sacrifice, payback for taking wild land into cultivation. The fungus persists as a forest predator, a destroyer of trees that remains unnoticed until it claims a victim. I wait until night and as the moon silvers the edges of clouds, I peer at the mushrooms and bootlaces on the rotting tree to see the bioluminescence honey fungus is noted for: cold-fire, fairy-fire, fox-fire, the weird-fire mentioned in the earliest surviving English poem, *Beowulf*. Whatever the speculation may be for the purpose of this bioluminescence, it remains a magic the fungus keeps to itself. However hard I stare at the sweet, earth-scented growths, I can only see a few spots of ghostly light like the luminous fragments of an old watchface.

The next day, along the old railway line, towers, domes and pinnacles rise from the wood's edge and the strange material of the city's architecture glows in sunlight. The structures which blossom in the air age quickly, decay and collapse while newer, bigger edifices heave out of the earth to replace them. Some are dark colours drawn from the underground, others more luminous and moonlike. Some are swept upwards on delicate pedestals, etched and frilled, others are lumpen hillocks. As if a subterranean civilisation struggles into the light only to extinguish itself, it is possible to observe the rise and fall of these ephemeral cities. Along these woods, the old track is closed at one end by a locked tunnel through the rock and at the other by private property and a road. There have been no trains for fifty years. The woods have closed in on the track and piles of long logs wait for collection. In the undergrowth between the track and the woods are colonies of fungi sending fruiting bodies out of the anarchic tangle of mycelium, webs of filament which stretch underground through the soil and plant roots. Some are saprotrophic, breaking down organic remains of stumps, sticks or leaves. Some are mycorrhizal, bonding with roots of trees or other plants in a relationship of mutual dependence. Some are parasitic, selecting trees they will kill. The fruiting bodies rise above ground to release spores. The life of fungi, on which we all depend, seems foreign to both animal and plant life – an existence which has infiltrated the world, a ghostly civilisation.

In *Invisible Cities*, Italo Calvino wrote about discovering cities from a past we did not know we had. The past was a place in which what we once had been and once possessed now lay in wait for us in foreign, unpossessed places. I look out into this country where my past stretches between hills, where I occupy the spaces between plants. I know it well but it will always be foreign to me and it would be wrong of me to pretend I had any proprietorial interest here. I cannot make any claim on this land. I un-possess it. What I see grows things in me like fungi, ephemeral yet recurring memories growing from an unconscious I share with this land. Fungal cities lie in wait through the woods. They rise and fall, sending spores like thoughts to travel into the future. We remember them from the past, familiar and strange at the same time.

Sunshine pours into Ape Dale, on its ripple of vivid fields, through its gaunt oaks, splashing across its gate puddles but wraiths of fog slide northwards up it, too. There is a pony and trap on the road pulled by a cob that looks as if he's clip-clopped out of the nineteenth century. There is a pied wagtail perching on a telephone wire through a blue sky. The wooded scarp of Wenlock Edge stands over the Dale, soaked in shadow, a black wave. Up in the woods, paths are claggy, others move along them: a man with a cudgel and no dog; men out rabbiting, one with an air rifle, one with a Jack Russell terrier and another with a ferret in a box; a lone crow chasing buzzards from the wood; rooks roistering in the ash tops; dark shapes doing ancient things. Out on Windmill Hill, the stallion screams. Something has spooked him. He gallops uphill at me with surprising speed for a stumpy little Shetland pony, threatening and kicking.

I ignore him and carry on so he returns to the other ponies, obviously freaked out. I pretend not to notice the buzzard flying out of a hedge so close I feel its wing-swish. I pretend not to notice the flock of fieldfares *whoosh* so low overhead. I ignore the sharp shower lobbed by a squall out of a blue sky but notice more is on the way. The build-up to this storm is a time of suddenness, rapid comings and goings, a gathering anxiety or excitement.

When it came, the storm dragged through the sky during the night and cleared the way for a bright sunny morning with fresh blue skies. Suddenly the light was turned on again and the landscape revealed itself with a new kind of shining confidence. This was characterised by a raven, flying in from the west towards the low winter sun, its glossy plumage reflecting the sunlight so that the bird shone, mirror-silvered, its long black wings flashing as they sculled across a still blue sky. But the stillness and brightness were not to last. Following the raven came a wind that strengthened, swinging along the wooded scarp of the Edge, hissing through the grey trunks of ash and the wine-red twigs of lime. Apart from the wind in the canopy, the woods were very quiet. Small birds were being pushed to the leeward edges but other ravens were riding or tacking across the wind.

The first voice sounds like the worn-out squeak of an old-fashioned toy repeatedly pressed by an owner who hasn't had enough of the joke yet. The second voice is a deep bass *kronk* from a throat which gargles sump oil. The voices of the ravens pass overhead. They are flying on the very edge – bright blue sky above them, pale grey murk below, as if swimming on the surface of a vast cloud which stretches the length of Wenlock Edge. The cloud laps around the Wrekin, turning it into a floating mountain, then hazes northwards into the plain and westwards to the Welsh hills blotting everything in a roll of cold smoke. Somewhere out there the lakes made by the River Severn in flood are creeping back to their beds like adulterers. Now there's just enough frost in the ground to stiffen the mud a bit and show where warmer, browner loam from below has been pushed out of molehills by the velvet subterraneans. Strung across pathways through the woods are tripwires of gossamer laid by spiders. Break them and a flash of sunlight bursts suddenly through trees. Charms of chaffinch and goldfinch bound between wood's edge and a field of thawing maize where pheasants rocket skyward as a blunt-headed dog crashes through the withered stalks.

A buzzard flies heavily around treetops which now stand clear of the fog. The bigger ash, beech and lime trees on the top of the Edge gradually emerge with a new clarity. Their forms are leafless, dark and elemental with a resurgent winter character which seems far from dormant but liberated from growth-making – a kind of life freed from the business of living. A lone raven lands in one of these trees: a big black bird in a big black tree framed against a bright blue sky as the fog thins to wisps. Its commanding bark echoes across fields, winter tricks out this landscape in the conjuror's voice. The conjuror flies overhead, sees me and swerves away, then half-turns back to get a better look. We meet at several points over a distance of a few miles. I call to it. It makes a few cryptic remarks in my direction. I imagine my calls convey some comradely recognition, a reassurance that I did not carry a gun or any harmful intentions; that

I celebrate the mythic status of ravens in this landscape from which they were purged and during my lifetime have returned in their hundreds. I imagine that if the raven's calls represent a piece of its mind, it won't be pretty: there is still illegal persecution, what my kind has done to this land is beneath contempt and perhaps we should go back to having bloody battles so ravens can feast on the slain. From the cliff at Major's Leap, the view across the Dale is greying, the wind shifts and another storm is on its way.

There is a small field where the sheep are so filthy they're indistinguishable from the mud they've trampled; they bleat and follow for food. There is a path over stiles into another wood where the water from Five Springs and the White Well gathers in sedgy beds under old coppiced alders. The path leads up a steep stepped bank below the witchy cackle of invisible redwings in the service trees or chequers. There is a place where the fallow deer go and there they are, black-backed and wary, leading the way to another place. And there – is a disaster. Four ancient lime pollards were once the boundary of the parish and its wood long before it spread out along fields too awkward to plough. For centuries the great fluted trunks of the limes must have been known, had names, were worked on and kept with sideways veneration. For a long time now they've been hidden, forgotten. Only the deer stay near them, to lay up in daytime, give birth in spring, fight in autumn. One old lime blew out in a storm two years ago. Now the largest, most hollow, most elephantine of them has been felled by the gale, its dark inner space smashed. A door is closed. The other two old limes will soon break up now the wind can worm into their grove. Soon none of them will stand, and all the things that don't matter and have been forgotten will go back where they came from.

In that place lies the cedar of Lebanon in the Wilderness at Powis Castle, huge old beech trees on Wenlock Edge, trees rotted through by fungi, *Phytophthora* or felled by chainsaws. There is a placeless place, beyond consciousness and the reach of culture, a forgotten forest as old as the one buried under the sands of Cardigan Bay. In it wander the forgotten souls who lived and worked this land: people like my great-uncle and those I served with in gardens and the wild animals that are scarcely imaginable now. There is a piece of dead lime wood the size of a dagger. It comes with me back through the woods.

A frost has fixed the leaves of ground ivy and moss and the sun is shining. White on green with fallen sallow leaves of purple and brown, this small patch, a plot no bigger than a newspaper page in a field of abandoned quarry scrape, has a radiant beauty. Its colours are so vivid and the connections between the living things and the way they inhabit the place creates a presence that has a strangely moving effect. The experience is not like looking at a painting or other image, it is part of a transitory sense of being part of a wild moment, a kind of spiritual gardening. This moment will last an hour until the frost thaws and the clouds return. Tomorrow it will be dark and pour with rain, and yet the same ground ivy and moss will be growing in the same spot, the sallow leaves will continue to rot and although each of these things will be beautiful, the absence of frost and sunlight will make this a different place. A sparrowhawk flicks over trees to land on the old iron pump which once drew water from the well. It settles, directing its forensic gaze from behind the weapon on its face, along the wall, down to the ground and into the hedge. The appearance of the hawk is sudden, as is most experiences of them. It is rare and thrilling to see the brown-banded feathers still, the grip of talons flex, to find myself in that glare. The hawk is looking: planning ways in, ways out, to snatch small birds from patches of sunlight. It pauses. The world slows to a standstill around the hawk as if all its speed has moved it through time and I am seeing something happening in the future; not a memory, a premonition. And as quickly as it arrived, the sparrowhawk is gone, to hunt the beating hearts of the present. And here they come. Small birds leave the sanctuary of hedges to occupy the space left by the hawk. Their movements are not random but choreographed by a shared intention; they are bound in this moment to each other and may not be so tomorrow. This is also true of a band of redwings, the sunset caught by their underwings as they fly together from the field into a sycamore. It is true of clusters of scarlet rose hips glowing before the redwings find them.

I'm not sure what catches my eye but I think it is the hole in a nut. When I look down, under overarching hazels, there is a litter of split shells on the ground, freshly worked, randomly scattered on the muddy track where it ducked into the wood from the lane. Grey squirrels have been rattling through the hazel coppice with stems thicker than arms reaching 15 feet to form a dense canopy. Such gnarled, old hazels are called 'derelict coppice' not having been worked by people for a generation or two. The term suggests a work ethic. For centuries hazel provided materials for building, furniture, fencing, gardening, charcoal as well as food. The cutting back to grow again is a process that shaped the character of woodland life. To some, coppicing is essential to woodland management and without it the woods would fall into neglect, disrepute, the conservation equivalent of moral turpitude. To foresters and those intent on standing in for Nature, a derelict coppice is a dereliction of duty; and the butterflies and wildflowers that flourish in the open woodland spaces created by coppicing are reason enough for that intrusive kind of management. However, in this neglected, disreputable little enclave of unmanaged hazel, there is a feeling of freedom from cultivation, a culture worked only by the wild things that inhabit it now.

I pick a hazelnut from the ground. It's a shiny, brown-as-a-nut brown and has a hole drilled into it. Looking carefully, the teeth marks at the edge of the hole are evidence that this is the work of a dormouse. Beautiful marks incised by the arboreal, nocturnal hazel dormouse, the invisible sprite of these woods. I saw one cross the road the other night, a little ginger streak risking all. I peer into the hole the dormouse crafted in the nut: a darkness, dream-space, sanctuary from chainsaws and axes of men; a time portal in which to hide from storms and history. A gift filled with luck, I put it in my pocket.

We turn slowly, like dogs settling down to sleep, into the winter solstice, the longest night. We dream and fragments of memory gather in abandoned corners of our fields like ground ivy and miniature forests of moss rimed with frost where fallen leaves shine before disintegrating – as if all this makes sense and has a reason and yet its beauty lies in its ephemeral almost-nothingness. Then we wake in another year. 'The days run away like wild horses over the hills,' said the poet Charles Bukowski. I look out from the woods of Wenlock Edge to the Shropshire Hills and Welsh Marches; the view I have studied and daydreamed over all my life; my plot, my place and story. There go the horses, moments which span no time at all, small wonders into the secret wilds.

SELECT BIBLIOGRAPHY

This is not a comprehensive list but a selection of works that helped me.

Calvino, I. (1972), (1997), *Invisible Cities*, Vintage, London

Clare, J., ed. John Goodridge (1995), *The Works of John Clare*, Wordsworth Editions, Ware

Clifford, S., King, A. (2006), *England in Particular: a celebration of the commonplace, the local, the vernacular and the distinctive*, Hodder & Stoughton, London

Frazer, J.G. (1922), (1929), *The Golden Bough: a study in magic and religion*, Macmillan, London

Graham, J. (2000), *Swarm*, Carcanet, Manchester

Graves, R. (1961), (1975), *The White Goddess: a historical grammar of poetic myth*, Faber & Faber, London

Hadfield, M. (1960), (1985), *A History of British Gardening*, Penguin Books, London

Heaney, S. (1969), (1972), *Door into the Dark*, Faber & Faber, London

Heidegger, M. (1971), trans. Alfred Hofstadter (1975), *Poetry, Language, Thought*, Harper & Row, New York

Hurlstone Jackson, K. (1951), (1971), *A Celtic Miscellany: translations from the Celtic literatures*, Penguin Books, Harmondsworth

James, A.R. et al. (2009), 'On optimal decision-making in brains and social insect colonies', *Journal of the Royal Society Interface*

Lethbridge, T.C. (1967), *A Step in the Dark*, Routledge & Kegan Paul, London

Lovelock, J. (2006), *The Revenge of Gaia*, Penguin Books, London

MacCaulay, R. (1953), (1966), *Pleasure of Ruins*, Walker and Co., Universal Digital Library

Margulis, M., Sagan, D. (2007), *Dazzle Gradually: reflections on the nature of nature*, Chelsea Green, White River Junction

Marren, P., Mabey, R. (2010), *Bugs Britannica*, Chatto & Windus, London

Mumford, W.F. (1977), *Wenlock in the Middle Ages*, Mumford, Shrewsbury

Nietzsche, F., trans. R.J. Hollingdale (1973), *Beyond Good and Evil*, Penguin Books, Harmondsworth

Nietzsche, F., trans. R.J. Hollingdale (1977), *A Nietzsche Reader*, Penguin Books, Harmondsworth

Oelschlaeger, M. (1991), *The Idea of Wilderness*, Yale University Press, New Haven

Perrin, J. (2013), *A Snow Goose & other utopian fictions*, Cinnamon Press, Blaenau Ffestiniog

Po, L., trans. David Hinton (1996), (1998), *The Selected Poems of Li Po*, Anvil Press, London

Ross, A. (1967), (1974), *Pagan Celtic Britain*, Cardinal, London

Thomas, K. (1984), *Man and the Natural World: changing attitudes in England 1500–1800*, Penguin Books, London

Thomas, R.S. (1973), (1986), *Selected Poems 1946–1968*, Bloodaxe Books, Newcastle upon Tyne

Toghill, P. (1990), (2006), *Geology of Shropshire*, Crowood Press, Marlborough

Various, ed. E.O. Wilson (1988), *Biodiversity*, National Academy Press, Washington DC

Various, trans. ed. Michael Alexander (1966), (2008), *The Wanderer: elegies, epics, riddles, poems of England's ancient origins*, Penguin Books, London

Wernham, C. et al. (2002), *The Migration Atlas: movements of the birds of Britain and Ireland*, T & A.D. Poyser, London, for BTO

Williamson, D. (2013), 'Larvae, Lophophores and Chimeras in Classification, Cell Development', *Biology* 2:128

Wilson, C. (1956), (2001), *The Outsider*, Phoenix, London

ACKNOWLEDGEMENTS

Like hedging and ditching, wandering around writing field notes is solitary work. Doing something with them, however, is wonderfully collaborative, so I want to thank those without whose help and support my work would be a compost heap of notebooks. Thanks to @Varvera for the drawings and Sue Lascelles for teasing this book out and editing; writerly support from John Vidal, Jim Perrin, Richard Kerridge and my fellow diarists and editors of the *Guardian* country diary; philosophical advice from Alan Holland and Jane Howarth; script advice from Sarah Blunt, Grant Sonnex and Brett Westwood of the BBC Natural History Unit Radio; journeys into aural landscapes with wildlife sound recordists Tom Lawrence and Chris Watson; inspirational science from Lynn Margulis, Don Williamson, Dave Evers and Ray Woods. Without my family I'm just some shadow in the mud and weeds, so I owe Nancy, Byron, Luby, Steve, Mia and Nona a gratitude I rarely show and to my parents, Naomi and George, who got me into all this in the first place. I don't know how to thank trees and birds and rocks and weathers and all the wild things, but I'll struggle to find a way. Oh, and Rosie, Skipper, Nina and Pru the dogs, too.